An Imperfect Leader

An Imperfect Leader

Human-Centered Leadership in (After) Action

Peter L. Stiepleman

ROWMAN & LITTLEFIELD
Lanham • Boulder • New York • London

Published by Rowman & Littlefield
An imprint of The Rowman & Littlefield Publishing Group, Inc.
4501 Forbes Boulevard, Suite 200, Lanham, Maryland 20706
www.rowman.com

86-90 Paul Street, London EC2A 4NE, United Kingdom

British Library Cataloguing in Publication Information Available

Library of Congress Cataloging-in-Publication Data

Names: Stiepleman, Peter L., 1975– author.
Title: An imperfect leader : human-centered leadership in (after) action / Peter L.
    Stiepleman.
Description: Lanham : Rowman & Littlefield, [2023] | Includes bibliographical
    references and index.
Identifiers: LCCN 2022059733 (print) | LCCN 2022059734 (ebook) | ISBN
    9781475871128 (cloth) | ISBN 9781475871135 (paperback) | ISBN
    9781475871142 (epub)
Subjects: LCSH: School superintendents—United States. | Educational leadership—
    United States.
Classification: LCC LB2831.72 .S78 2023 (print) | LCC LB2831.72 (ebook) | DDC
    371.2/011—dc23/eng/20230210
LC record available at https://lccn.loc.gov/2022059733
LC ebook record available at https://lccn.loc.gov/2022059734

♾™ The paper used in this publication meets the minimum requirements of American
National Standard for Information Sciences—Permanence of Paper for Printed Library
Materials, ANSI/NISO Z39.48-1992.

For the children of trailer C.
The seeds you planted in my mind took root and showed me the way.

Contents

Preface

AN IMPERFECT LEADER: WHO TELLS YOUR STORY?

The real secret to a fabulous life is to live imperfectly with great delight.

—Leigh Standley

Every year at the breakfast for new teachers, I would welcome nearly 150 new educators to the school district. We always started with our assistant superintendent for human resources, who announced that we received nearly two thousand applications for positions, which represented the best of the best. The chamber of commerce soon followed with their own welcome.

I always valued their remarks because they were quick to highlight the economic impact of the school district, the third largest employer in the city. They would say something like "when the school district thrives, people want to live here. When people want to live here, homes and restaurants need to be built. When these new businesses take root, property taxes bring new revenues to the school district. Sometimes the growth means new school buildings will be needed."

Although this often goes over the heads of the new teachers because they are so nervous about being new (and are more focused on the biscuits and gravy waiting for them at the end of these opening speeches), I appreciated the reminder of the importance of a school district in a community's economy.

Following breakfast, it was my turn. I gave the superintendent's welcome, in which I always spoke of my first teaching experience in trailer C in Oakland, California. Most years I spoke of the children in my class and what they taught me. Sometimes, though, I told a different story. I told them a story about lessons learned after a brush with chaos.

During my first year of teaching in a Spanish bilingual classroom in Oakland, California, our school adopted a reading program that required children to go to another classroom for ninety minutes each morning for reading instruction. Depending on student needs, teachers were assigned different reading levels. One grading period, I taught sixth-grade English to fourth and fifth graders. It was in this reading class that I learned a valuable lesson.

Our classroom, made up almost exclusively of advanced students from other classrooms, came to trailer C each morning. I selected Mildred Taylor's *Roll of Thunder, Hear My Cry*. I still remember the spirited conversations about race, class, and their intersectionality in the Deep South during the early part of the twentieth century.

Every morning, we started the lesson with five vocabulary words. I encouraged the children to act out the words using a second language learning strategy called total physical response (TPR). I thought this strategy would help the students remember those important words or phrases, which language acquisition experts refer to as "brick and mortar" words.

On this fateful morning, I selected my words and the children acted them out. I would count to three and they'd begin. To get them ready for the next word, I simply announced the next word was coming. One word I remember clearly was *prowl*. The hunched children tiptoed as they prowled around the classroom. I think another word was *pout* or *mope* or *scowl*. Whatever it was, I remember them looking sad and forlorn (there may have even been a few whimpers). Then it was time for the next word, a word I will never forget.

Without establishing a shared image of what acting out the word could look like and without declaring my expectations, I announced the next word. *Chaos*. I counted, "One, two, three!" I still have nightmares about what I witnessed.

My advanced reading students trashed my classroom. They toppled desks. They pulled down the posters. They tossed books and stood on chairs. They fully acted out the word *chaos*.

They couldn't hear me yelling to stop. I ran to the wall and flicked the lights on and off. This got their attention. I marched to the front of the room and hollered, "What is wrong with you? You're acting like a bunch of jackasses!" To this a student looked at me and said, "I don't appreciate you calling me a jackass." I thought about debating whether I called them jackasses or said they were acting *like* jackasses. Either way, it would have been a losing proposition.

What I can tell you is that we spent the rest of the class acting out the phrase "clean up this mess." I will never forget the faces of my students when they returned from their reading classrooms. "¿*Qué pasó*? What happened?" And I will never forget the other teachers, my colleagues, whose advanced readers had returned to their classrooms eager to share that they had been called jackasses! One saw me taking my class to lunch, gave me a smirk, and said, "Soooo, how was *your* morning?"

I learned a lot from this awful teaching moment. I learned about setting expectations, showing positive examples, and establishing a signal for when things were getting out of control. I told this story to remind new teachers that they would make mistakes, and that it was OK. What's important is that you learn from your mistakes. And share them with others so they will learn, too. That's what this book is all about. This is a series of stories, decisions, and reflections experienced by a superintendent over several years. It is a book about the superintendency, leadership, and understanding through the power of storytelling.

Storytelling

When I was a teacher, I used story to teach my lessons. The curriculum became relevant when there was a compelling story associated with the learning. The same was true when I was a principal. Every single Monday, I would tell a story that served almost like a sermon. It was always a reminder that when you crossed the threshold into our building, you had permission to be a child. This was not necessarily easy in a school where nearly 90 percent of the children participated in the National School Lunch Program and where they were often the caretakers while their parents worked two (or more) low-wage jobs without benefits.

Nearly all leaders craft a narrative to help define their organizations and its values and to establish a compelling purpose driven by a moral focus. Linda Henke, the director of the Santa Fe Center for Transformational School Leadership, notes in *Language as Vision*, "One of the most powerful tools of transformational leaders is language. Our use of language shapes to a large extent the way people see us, how much they trust us, and how willing they are to commit themselves to the work we share."[1]

Henke also stresses the important relationship between leadership and storytelling. "Story," she wrote, "triggers emotions and connections that are seldom accessed in other kinds of language."[2]

Who Tells Your Story?

In 2015, Lin-Manuel Miranda's musical *Hamilton* took the country by storm. While my children reenacted the cabinet duels in our living room every night, I was thinking about our school district and its story. It occurred to me that before superintendents could talk adequately about leadership and lessons learned, they need to consider their own stories: who they are, where they came from, and how their experiences shaped their moral focus and decision-making processes. I am from "Across the Sea," Martin D., and trailer C.

Across the Sea

My grandfather, Jacow Stipelman, arrived at Ellis Island on June 26, 1912. Jacow, who later took the name Jack Stiepleman (and Jack Steele to better assimilate in his new country), came to the United States from Odessa, in modern-day Ukraine. To have stayed in his shtetl would have meant certain death. After the Russian Revolution in 1905, Black Hundreds targeted Jews in raids known as pogroms. My grandfather and his parents *had* to leave Odessa. They risked everything to get on a boat named *Russia* so that they could build a better life in the United States.

In 2013, my wife and I took our three boys to the mouth of the Black Sea in Istanbul, Turkey. We stood high on a bluff, and I exclaimed, "Boys! One hundred years ago, my grandfather, *your* great-grandfather, risked everything to get to America. He risked everything so that we, his descendants, could have a better life. Just think about it: Odessa is directly north of here, in Ukraine. Imagine what he'd be thinking right now if he could see us, here, in Istanbul, on *vacation*!"

I am from across the sea.

Martin D

Martin David Ginsburg was my uncle. Aside from his tax law skills, what made him special was his ability to cook. The ability to cook may not seem like a remarkable achievement, but my two brothers and I credit our Uncle Martin for actively challenging traditional gender roles. The three of us love to cook and actively take on cooking responsibilities. His influence extended beyond cooking, too. I credit him with the maxim: "There are no magic gnomes in your homes." Whenever I tell my story and relate the influence Martin had on my life, I say, "There are no magic gnomes in your homes. If you discover the meals in your home have been prepared, the laundry has been done, and your children are well cared for, and *you* haven't done much of the work, then you'd better consider who *is* doing the work. There are no magic gnomes in your homes."

I am from Martin D. Ginsburg.

Trailer C

I wasn't an education major. I was a Spanish major with an international affairs minor because I thought I would pursue a career in foreign service and become an ambassador. I worked at the U.S. Embassy in Madrid, Spain, in the tourism division and the economic development division, where I connected U.S. exporters with Spanish importers.

After I graduated from college, I moved to Oakland, California, and followed in my father's footsteps by working for an insurance company in San Francisco. One day, a postcard arrived at my house inviting me to participate in "Drop Everything and Read Day." Instead of going to work one morning, I instead went to a third-grade classroom in Berkeley and read a book to children and answered questions about my job. I read *The Beggar's Magic*, a children's book written by Margaret and Raymond Chang.[3]

I remember how engaged the children were and how alive I felt as I read the story with its warning not to be stingy like mean old Farmer Wu. I remember how touched I was that the children sang to me and how tickled I was when the tempo their teacher had chosen was a bit too fast, leaving their version of "Take the A Train" essentially a runaway train. It was more of a jazz scat of the Duke Ellington classic.

Immediately afterward, I rushed past the Transamerica building and back to my cubicle. I quickly discovered that the State of California was desperate for teachers, especially bilingual teachers, and I immediately enrolled in the University of California-Berkeley CALPIP Program. It was the most important decision I would ever make.

I'll never forget my very first day at Allendale Elementary School. It was 1998, and I walked into the office carrying a box of school supplies. I noticed a sign over the desk of the principal's secretary: *A lack of planning on your part does not constitute an emergency on mine.* I was not to be deterred. I was too excited to be distracted by such an off-putting sign. "I'm your new third-grade teacher!" I proudly announced.

No one seemed very impressed. I later learned that there was such a revolving door of new teachers in the Flatlands (the Hills are where much of Oakland's influence and affluence live) that a new teacher was a common occurrence. The secretary gave me a set of keys and told me I'd be teaching in trailer C. "Where is trailer C?" I asked. She turned her head, her glasses resting on the tip of her nose as she looked down at me. She said, "It's between trailer B and trailer D."

I found trailer C, and it was in that space where my life would change forever. I may have been raised in New York, but it was in the Oakland Unified School District where I grew up and more fully observed the inequities strangling cities across the nation.

Oakland, at the time, was a moderately large city with four hundred thousand residents. Extremely diverse, its neighborhoods, however, remained ethnic and linguistic enclaves. The city administered more than one hundred elementary (grades K–5), middle (grades 6–8), and high schools (grades 9–12). There were several small autonomous schools and charter schools.

Allendale was a year-round urban elementary school with 650 students— more than 70 percent identified as English learners, children whose first language was not English. The school was surrounded by residential homes and apartment complexes. A few blocks from a major freeway, the school had a lot of car and truck traffic. Grocery shopping was limited to any number of corner stores.

The school was an older structure that had been on the modernization wait-list for several years. A few years after I moved to another elementary school, Allendale *did* get a stand-alone addition, which included additional classrooms so that children could attend a traditional school year (previously, the school's enrollment was 650, but only 500 could attend at any given time due to space issues). Signs of the building's age were apparent, and the toilets were in constant need of servicing, something the parents reminded the administration about daily. The school had seven portable classrooms. Trailer C was mine.

Overall, the classrooms had seen little improvement since they were constructed. Some had been equipped with whiteboards (as replacements to the traditional blackboards). The school was habitually without classroom supplies of soap or paper towels. The administration distributed hand sanitizers to promote healthy habits.

I taught a Spanish bilingual class in trailer C. Each morning, I greeted children at the entrance. Standing there, I shared a moment with each child to get a sense of how the day would go and to see who needed a little extra care. Each day, I was introduced to their lives, their hopes, and their dreams.

Let me introduce you to six of them. (The names of the children are pseudonyms.)

Gabriel was brought to the United States as a child, his parents searching for better opportunities. Gabriel was incredibly smart, and he told me he wanted to be a lawyer so that he could help the families in his neighborhood (like his) navigate an unaccommodating system.

Alejandro didn't start in my classroom. One day, he stood at the entrance of trailer C with a note. I walked over and took it from him. It said, "Alejandro is in *your* classroom now." I had no idea a colleague could just decide a child was no longer in her classroom! I soon learned that Alejandro was an exceptional child with a different learning style.

He taught me to find ways to teach concepts and skills. I had no idea whether to explore special education services for him (or whether that would be appropriate). One day, apropos of nothing, he declared, "I have hair on my ass." We all learned to expect and accept Alejandro's "contributions" to class discussions.

Eugenia was the younger daughter of two incredibly hard-working parents. When Eugenia's father wasn't pouring tar on roofs, he was removing asbestos from buildings. When her mother wasn't cleaning homes, she was caring for the children who lived in those homes. Eugenia's parents lived in a very small, dark first floor apartment. I was invited over once and remarked on the tiny window, which allowed only a thin line of sunlight. It reminded me of how Deborah Ellis described Parvana's Kabul apartment in *The Breadwinner*.[4]

America was talented. She was intelligent, curious, and hungry to learn everything. Her family was Jehovah's Witness, which required active participation in the congregation. America was comfortable reading a text and separating out the plot from the message. She knew how to draw conclusions and cite evidence from the text to back up her positions.

I was determined to help America and thought that help was in the form of sponsorship to a private school. My wife's family and my family helped her get a scholarship, and we paid the remaining tuition. She stayed for two years and then returned to the Oakland Public Schools. When I asked her why she came back, she told me, "I didn't understand their lives and they couldn't understand mine."

At that moment, I realized how wrong I was. We should do everything we can to make leaving public schools the hardest decision. Public schools should be a beacon for every family in every community. What I had done was raise a white flag on public schools instead of putting my energy into making public education the very best. What I had done was essentially provide a voucher to a family. America's family didn't need a voucher. They needed the Oakland Unified School District to provide an extraordinary education to their child.

Javier was the reason I wrote my dissertation on why children learn or don't learn English. Here was an agreeable kid who loved to joke around with his friends and collect Pokémon cards. He came across as a confident child, especially with his command of English. When it came to academic English, however, he struggled. When I learned about how children were assigned to bilingual or English-only classrooms, I was startled that the system was designed to balance enrollment numbers.

It began my real interest in system design and system thinking. It prompted me to write this book because I believe leaders will achieve better results when they've considered the systems they've inherited, the systems they've created, and the systems they are determined to change.

Isaiah will never know how profoundly he changed my life. His mother paid a coyote—someone who smuggles immigrants from Mexico into the United States—to take her and her two young sons to Oakland, where they could reunite with her husband and the boys' father. The first time she made the desert crossing, they were detained. Isaiah's mother described to me how she would not let go of her child. She was being urged to let go of her son and to run from the authorities, who were close in pursuit. She and her boys were caught and sent back to Mexico. During her second attempt, she and her boys made it to Los Angeles, where they took a bus to Oakland. They had romanticized what the reunion was going to be like. Tragically, it was a nightmare. Every night, Isaiah, his mother, his little brother, and their dog slept in a closet while his father drank and played cards.

My own father always told me that to whom we are born involves luck. We don't get a choice. There isn't some selection process where you get to say, "I choose to be born into an abusive situation." "I choose to be poor." "I choose to struggle." For all of us born into healthy situations without any significant struggles, we have an obligation to help others.

When my wife and I were expecting our first child, we intentionally named him after Isaiah. Every day, when we saw our child, we would be reminded to work harder for all children, not just some.

I am also from trailer C.

It is critical that I tell my stories. They influenced the kind of leader I wanted to be. They were my foundation. They inspired and fueled what had become my moral focus. They informed my compelling purpose, the inclusion of experiences to inspire children to aspire to the lives their parents dreamed of for them. Tipping over bookshelves, filling them with soil, planting a variety of seeds, and setting up grow lights allowed us to sponsor the Great Bean Olympics. Collecting milk containers and yarn cones provided the materials to construct a replica of Oakland for a trash-to-treasure show. Caring for crayfish and tending to chrysalides created opportunities to witness the life cycle in real life. These experiences promoted curiosity and learning, two traits I associate with the power of human-centered leading, where teachers and leaders serve as activators of learning.

I identify as a human-centered leader and having an opportunity to learn from my experiences is fundamental to that identity. In this book, you join a superintendent on his journey. The stories you encounter have been carefully selected. Sharing with you the experiences of a superintendent is essential. It is my sincere desire that this book gives you an opportunity to learn from his experiences as you continue to develop your leadership skills, because they speak to a reality: the imperfection of leadership.

Imperfect Leader

When you hear the word *imperfect*, think about the images that come to mind. Until I began writing this book, I must admit that what came to mind for me was incompetence. There's a difference between incompetent and imperfect. So much of the professional literature presented to leaders is the curation of a perfect image, but we all are imperfect. Perfect scenario after perfect scenario leads one to believe they're deficient. But when you experience someone else's mistakes, you relate to them, and your takeaway is a feeling of being seen.

If you were looking for a book that celebrated perfection, then this book is not for you. This is a book about imperfection. It's about an imperfect leader striving to learn from his experiences through genuine reflection. This book is an examination of decisions and a deconstruction of some lessons learned. The aim of this book is to lift the learning and to lift the imperfect leaders. That way, when you hear the term *imperfect*, you'll see strength, strength from the candor needed to recognize imperfection as a real advantage.

NOTES

1. Linda Henke, *Leaders' Learning Work: The Language of Vision* (St. Louis: Washington University Institute for School Partnership, 2017).

2. Henke, *Leaders' Learning Work*.

3. Margaret Scrogin Chang and Raymond Chang, *The Beggar's Magic* (New York: M. K. McElderry Books, 1997).

4. Deborah Ellis, *The Breadwinner* (Toronto: Douglas & McIntyre, 2001).

Acknowledgments

This book is an exploration into the decisions of a superintendent from the hiring process through the global pandemic. Writing a book about the experiences of a superintendent and documenting his reflections required vulnerability, and I feel privileged to bring them to you, the reader.

I am first and foremost indebted to Tom Koerner and the entire Rowman & Littlefield Publishing team for seeing value in this authentic story. I want to thank David Wilson for being my thought partner during the entire project and to Sean Doherty and Mark Miles, two superior superintendents, for reading and helping me revise the very first after-action review I ever wrote. I am grateful to Tim Hill for editing the manuscript before it went to the publisher. A deep and heartfelt acknowledgment goes to Tracy Benson and the Waters Center for Systems Thinking for generating system-thinking trainings and tools so that leaders can consider complex decisions in a very deliberate and thoughtful manner.

This project never would have come to fruition if it hadn't been for Linda Henke, my mentor and friend. I am grateful for the trust she gave me with the leadership model she created, a model that challenges leaders to rethink top-down hierarchies and embrace shared decision making in a very human-centered way.

Finally, to my family. The phrase *l'dor vador*—from generation to generation—makes an appearance in this book. Each time I wrote it, I thought of the Chayat, Stiepleman, Bayer, and Ginsburg families. I thought of their sacrifices and how they modeled *simcha*, *tzedakah*, and *shalom*. To my parents, Ed and Claire, my in-laws, Margaret and Raymond, to my brothers, David and Daniel, and sisters-in-law, Carey and Jess, thank you for always supporting me. To my wife, Elizabeth Chang, and our children, Isaac, Ezra, and Jacob, thank you for your enduring love and encouragement.

Chapter 1

Theory of Action

Each journey is unique, and each seeker charts a new path. But it is infinitely easier to do so having at least some knowledge about the experiences of those who have gone before.

—Carol Pearson

Leaders are led not only by their experiences, but also by the experiences and writings of others. This book is influenced by a belief that access eliminates both opportunity and achievement gaps, that human-centered leadership can transform systems, and that system thinking helps leaders make more predictably successful decisions.

THIS I BELIEVE

National Public Radio hosts a weekly radio essay called *This I Believe*. Anyone can submit their reflections on anything from world affairs to life, work, or family, and the project's curator selects one for the broader listening audience. Superintendents are often asked what they believe, to speak of their vision.

In so many urban school districts around the nation, curricular areas like music, art, physical education, and science were the responsibility of the classroom teacher. Recess was supervised by classroom teachers as well. When school leaders begin considering why some children achieve and others do not, one logical conclusion is that it has to do with opportunity gaps.

If you grew up as a middle-class kid, it is more likely that you took music lessons and played on local soccer and baseball teams. You likely visited museums and attended live performances in nearby cities. If you were middle class, you were introduced to the world in a remarkably different way than your peers growing up in poverty. You might even have thought for a good part of your youth that everyone had had those same experiences. If you were middle class, you learned new vocabulary and embraced new experiences.

There is a theory of action in this book. If the superintendent writing this book were the focus of a *This I Believe* segment, he might recognize his beliefs to be rooted in the work of Jim Cummins and Richard Rothstein. He would recognize how their work has influenced him as an educator and as a leader.

Jim Cummins believes that underrepresented groups are either empowered or disabled by educators. He concludes that the achievement gap could be closed if schools were to consider four important elements: cultural/linguistic incorporation, community participation, pedagogy, and assessments. Cummins argues that if educators rethink the way that they teach underrepresented groups and move away from a "rhetoric of equality and the reality of domination," then students from the dominated group would stand a chance in a dominating society.[1]

Richard Rothstein urges schools to consider how the achievement gap is directly linked to an enrichment gap.[2] He argues that middle-class children are introduced to far more enrichment activities compared to their poorer peers and, as a result, use these experiences to excel in school. This is why leaders in high-poverty schools make efforts to arrange field trips to museums and the symphony. It is why they apply for grants for artists and conservationists and musicians to come teach and perform. It is why the children in their schools learn how to read music and perform concerts for the whole school. It is why they start choirs and, with the help of local community groups, launch instrumental bands.

It is why they get creative with parent engagement. One teacher in a California school held parent-teacher conferences at professional baseball games and took the entire grade (and their parents) on overnight campouts and day trips to the Pacific Coast.

Cummins reminds us that courageous conversations are essential in prompting a system to support all children. Rothstein reminds us that when we enhance the learning opportunities for every child, we see the true development of the whole child. As leaders, we look at the wisdom of Cummins and Rothstein, and we can see they are advocating for achievement and enrichment. They are pushing for opportunities. They believe in access for all, not some.

HUMAN-CENTERED SCHOOL
TRANSFORMATION MODEL

Have you ever gone overnight camping? I don't particularly love camping, but I *do* like going hiking in the woods. Once, when I went overnight camping with my wife on the California coast, she woke up in the middle of the night thinking birds were eating all our food. In the morning, we unzipped our tent to find—well—that birds had eaten all our food (though they *did* leave us the powdered coffee and a dented can of tuna). So, no, I don't love camping, but I do love going on hikes in the woods.

Why am I telling you this? Well, when I am asked to describe the leadership model I believe in the most, I turn to what I believe to be the most complete model: the human-centered school transformation model (see figure 1.1).[3] It is an approach that values people first and foremost. It also accepts that we all get better when we are continually learning. It is a model that organizations don't easily follow because it compels leaders to share leadership, which is the opposite of traditional top-down leadership approaches.

In fact, in conversations I've had with leaders in other fields, I am convinced it would be a powerful model for business leaders, nonprofit executives, hospital administrators, and at every level of local, state, and national government. If you allow me to stick with the hiking metaphor, I'll explain the model.

At the beginning of any hike is an entrance called a trailhead. The trailhead is the start of your trip and almost always provides a map to your

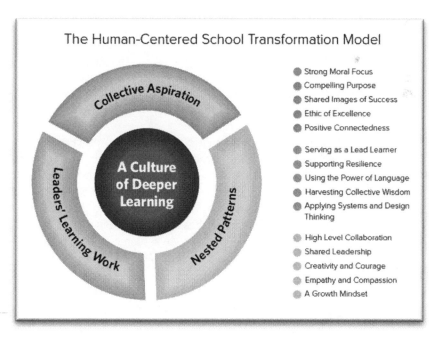

Figure 1.1. Human-Centered School Transformation Model.
Source: Dr. Linda Henke, Santa Fe Center for School Transformation.

destination—whether it be a waterfall, a lake, or a campsite (yech). The human-centered school transformation model has three trailheads, which all lead to a place where everyone is honored and valued, where everyone plays an important part—these trailheads lead to a culture of deep learning. A culture of deep learning is a different way to think about leadership. It asks you to think about the *why*, the *what*, and the *how* of leading in a different way. Those three trailheads are known as collective aspiration, nested patterns, and leaders' learning work.

- *Collective aspiration* ensures that everyone in the organization is on the same page and that everyone is working toward the same goal. If we all aspire toward the same thing and share the same understanding of what success looks like, then it is more likely we will succeed. Collective aspiration is the heart of everything that is done.[4] When someone is unclear as to why a decision has been made or an approach is being considered, collective aspiration serves as the *why*.
- *Nested patterns* are the behaviors of everyone in the organization and describe the behaviors that are valued. Nested patterns include people working together and collaborating. They include sharing leadership responsibilities and emphasizing the importance of creativity, courage, empathy, and compassion. Nested patterns are the trailhead that challenges individuals to be critical about the way they've always seen the world. In the human-centered school transformation model, nested patterns are the muscle of the work. Just as musicians or athletes practice and practice so their motions become automatic, leaders who learn these nested patterns understand *what* it means to lead. Nested patterns are important when things are going well, and they are *essential* when things are not going so well.
- *Leaders' learning work* is where core processes and practices can be found. It is where we are reminded of the fundamentals of leadership. For one, that leadership is about showing others that you're willing to admit you've made mistakes and then showing how you've learned from those mistakes. It is also about using everyone's ideas to design a better way of doing things and adjusting those systems when necessary. And it is being able to communicate ideas in a way that everyone can understand. Leaders' learning work is the *how*. It is the brains of the work.

Collective aspiration, nested patterns, and leaders' leading work each lead us to that better place as an organization. They are the trailheads, or dimensions, that lead to a culture of deep learning.

HUMAN-CENTERED SCHOOL TRANSFORMATION MODEL RESOURCES

Santa Fe Center for Transformational School Leadership:
https://transformationalschoolleadership.com

SYSTEMS THINKING

In this book, we explore the experiences of the superintendent of a moderately large school district. In one situation, he was faced with an issue. His school district had begun trying to look at equity and equitable practices in a new way, and it had to confront past practices that served as real obstacles. The work up until this point was mostly episodic, with conversations around equity attracting those who already believed in the work.

The school district invited Doug Reeves to talk about the case against the zero when it came to giving grades.[5] The school district hosted Anthony Muhammad to discuss collaborative work called professional learning communities and how to minimize those who would choose to undermine such efforts.[6] The school district's task force met periodically to discuss issues of inequitable practices, but there wasn't a system-wide approach to equity until the chief academic officer began stitching a relationship with nationally recognized organizations like the Minority Student Achievement Network[7] and AVID.[8] It was then that they started designing a more responsive system.

One example of a more system-wide focus occurred in the math department. The math sequence in high school followed this order: algebra 1, geometry, algebra 2. Middle school gifted students who wished to enroll in these courses were given that option, but it created an inequitable system. It was fine from a scheduling standpoint for sixth graders to enroll in algebra 1, because there were seventh and eighth graders also taking this course. It was also OK when, as seventh graders, they enrolled in geometry, because there were eighth graders enrolled in this course.

The issue, in what could be only described as opportunity hoarding,[9] occurred when five children enrolled in algebra 2 (two of whom were bused over from another middle school). This meant the school district would allocate a math teacher for these five children (plus pay for a daily shuttle bus), leaving more than thirty students in a regular math class. The superintendent's son was one of those five. For years, children were enrolled in these higher-level courses while depriving their peers of getting more personal attention.

THE WATERS CENTER FOR SYSTEMS THINKING

Founded by Jim and Faith Waters, the Waters Center for Systems Thinking[10] is an organization dedicated to helping individuals and institutions make better decisions. Many leaders are familiar with using the metaphor of an iceberg when thinking about a problem. The Waters Center encourages individuals to see what is happening (the visible part of the iceberg) as well as the mental models (the perspectives of people, how they've been socialized), the structure of the system (every system is designed to do *exactly* what it was designed to do), and the patterns of behavior (how the actions of the people in the system influence what happens).

The Waters Center for Systems Thinking helps leaders consider multiple perspectives and more. Their collection of Habits of a Systems Thinker cards prompt leaders to design systems to help make more thoughtful decisions. In the case of offering a math class to very few students, the "big picture" habit card would have been a good way to think about whether the school should have offered the course. When leaders *seek to understand the big picture*, they make better decisions. In this situation, the school district had seen the tree and not the forest.

At the end of each chapter of this book, there are prompts from a Habits of a System Thinker card. Readers are encouraged to review them, think about problems of practice facing them, and answer them individually or with their teams. They're great tools for leaders at every level.

WATERS CENTER FOR SYSTEM THINKING RESOURCES

Habits of a Systems Thinker cards:
https://thinkingtoolsstudio.waterscenterst.org/cards

AFTER-ACTION REVIEW

In public education, superintendents and building leaders are often hired because they were good teachers. They then move up the chain of command to the point at which they have become CEOs of large organizations. For example, an elementary school principal of three hundred children and thirty staff can easily become the superintendent of nearly twenty thousand children and three thousand staff members. Superintendents must shift from relational leaders to systems leaders, and they have to learn a lot of this on the job.

Additionally, superintendents don't engage in an after-action review (AAR)[11] process as a regular course of action because (a) they haven't been trained to do so and (b) they are running from one high-stakes decision to the next. They have little to no time to genuinely reflect on their decisions, even though that's where the greatest learning takes place. The military conducts these protocols routinely. Hospital administrators, too. Superintendents are like those two professions in a lot of ways for their diplomacy skills and hands-on, compassionate care. Reviewing what happened and learning from the experience should not be a luxury, but a regular course of action.

Linda Lambert (2019) wrote:

> How mistakes are handled is a major stimulant for learning and provides salient insight into the character of the leader as well. When a "leader" doesn't take responsibility for his or her mistakes, or becomes angry and defensive if they are pointed out, this individual is incapable of becoming an excellent leader or learner.[12]

I believe that schools (all organizations, really) need to seek out ways to promote reflection, which will result in the creation of community. The community Lambert writes about is defined as "the reciprocal processes that enable participants in an educational community to construct meanings that lead toward a common purpose of schooling."[13] That is achieved, she adds, by moving "outside of oneself, to differentiate one's perceptions from those of another, to practice empathy, to move out of the self and observe the responses and thoughts of another."

Throughout my time as a building leader and district leader, I wrote personal reflections that I often shared in a weekly newsletter. The following entry complements Linda Lambert's wisdom:

> It has never been harder to be a public servant. I've been reading the Ulysses S. Grant biography and I've been wondering to myself how successful he would have been had social media been a thing during the 1860s. How would he have responded to online petitions and the constant barrage of emails? His handwritten letters to President Lincoln took days and weeks to arrive in Washington, D.C., and then took weeks to months for a response. I'm certainly not being wistful for the days of forced conscription, but there is something nice to think that there was once a time when leaders could truly process and think about the best course of action. They could read, write, and reflect in advance of making a thoughtful decision.

In each remaining chapter of this book, a scenario is unpacked, a single issue from a superintendent's perspective, with an after-action review to explore:

- What happened?
- What got overlooked?
- What was learned about relationships?
- What was frustrating?
- What could have been done differently?
- What was something good that came out of this experience?

Over the course of the book, from the process of being named superintendent to leading during a global pandemic, you will observe examples of how an imperfect leader used his past experiences to become a better leader.

WATERS CENTER FOR SYSTEMS THINKING HABIT

A Leader Changes Perspectives to Increase Understanding

The rest of this book asks readers to consider the experiences of others as well as their own.

As you learn about new perspectives, what are some ways you work intentionally to challenge your thinking?

NOTES

1. Jim Cummins, "Pedagogies of Choice: Challenging Coercive Relations of Power in Classrooms and Communities," *International Journal of Bilingual Education and Bilingualism* 12 (2009): 261–71.

2. Richard Rothstein, "The Racial Achievement Gap, Segregated Schools, and Segregated Neighborhoods: A Constitutional Insult," *Race and Social Problems* 7, no. 1 (2014): 21–30.

3. "A Model for Human-Centered School Transformation," Santa Fe Center for Transformational School Leadership, https://transformationalschoolleadership.com/transformationleadership/model-for-human-centered-school-transformation.

4. Linda Henke was the first to describe collective aspiration as the *heart* of the work, nested patterns as the *muscle* of the work, and leaders' learning work as the *brains* of the work.

5. Douglas B. Reeves, "The Case against the Zero," *Phi Delta Kappan* 86, no. 4 (2004): 324–25.

6. Anthony Muhammad, *Transforming School Culture: How to Overcome Staff Division* (Bloomington, IN: Solution Tree Press, 2018).

7. "MSAN Network," Minority Student Achievement Network, http://msan .wceruw.org.

8. "AVID/Closing the Achievement Gap in Education," Advancement via Individual Determination, www.avid.org.

9. Sean Kelly and Heather Price, "The Correlates of Tracking Policy," *American Educational Research Journal* 48, no. 3 (2016): 560–85.

10. Waters Center for Systems Thinking, https://waterscenterst.org.

11. "After-Action Review," Wikipedia, https://en.wikipedia.org/wiki/After-action _review.

12. Linda Lambert, *Leaders as Lead Learners* (Santa Fe, NM: Santa Fe Center for Transformational School Leadership, 2019), 11.

13. Linda Lambert, "Leadership Redefined: An Evocative Context for Teacher Leadership," *School Leadership & Management* 23, no. 4 (2013): 421–30.

Chapter 2

A Challenge to Stasis

Life is a series of natural and spontaneous changes. Don't resist them—
that only creates sorrow. Let reality be reality. Let things flow naturally
forward in whatever way they like.

—Lao Tzu

What happened?
The superintendent selection process.
What got overlooked?
The importance of understanding where you've been as part of chart-
ing a course for where you're going.
What was learned about relationships?
Relationships can be transactional.
What was frustrating?
Expecting the selection to be based on a vision for the school district
and learning that was not the case for some board members.
What could have been done differently?
Dedicating time to listen and learn should never be overlooked.
What was something good that came out of this experience?
An understanding about how to begin building relationships within
the organization.

In 1946, in a small Midwest university town, Neil Aslin was hired as the
superintendent of schools. He led the school district for sixteen years, until
1962. His successor, Bob Shaw, served the next fourteen years until his retirement in 1976. These two leaders led the school district during a significant
period in the nation's history. World War II had just ended, the Korean War
was on the horizon, and with *Brown v. Board of Education of Topeka*, the

Supreme Court decided "separate but equal" was most definitely not constitutional. Following the court's ruling, Dr. Aslin faced pushback from the community. Families at an elementary school protested when their school had to accept eleven African American children. In fact, the parents at this school canceled their annual chili supper because they feared African American parents would plan to attend as well. A meeting was held with the president of the National Association for the Advancement of Colored People, who agreed to "recommend to the black families involved that they not attend the chili supper."[1]

In my conversations with leaders across the country, and certainly in my experiences, when a disruption is presented, the system works aggressively to return to stasis. This appeared to be the case in 2003 with the hiring of Dr. Phyllis Chase, the school district's first African American superintendent. Dr. Chase was qualified to lead the school district, having served as the director of curriculum in Topeka, Kansas, assistant superintendent and acting superintendent in Kansas City, Missouri, and chief of staff in Springfield, Missouri. Dr. Chase understood curriculum and she was aware of Columbia's achievement gaps. She should have been credited with convening the Achievement Gap Task Force, which was the precursor to what would later become known as District Equity Teams. She should have been credited for having the courage to establish The Model School, where she completely overhauled an underperforming elementary school located less than a mile from her office. She should have been credited with disrupting the status quo. Instead, following a publicly criticized land purchase for a new high school and a failed tax levy election, she resigned from her position and was erased from the district's narrative. She was replaced by a retired superintendent, a leader with a close connection to the superintendents who had led the school district since 1946.

School leaders often look back on their careers and think about their path to the superintendency. Sometimes, they recall a crisis that propelled them into the position. Others benefited from being part of a clear succession plan. And often, there is notification of a retirement, a selection process coordinated by the school board, community presentations, and a job offer. The following story follows that scenario. What we glean from this experience is that even seemingly simple processes are never simple.

A school district's assistant superintendent was out of town attending a math conference when he received the news. The superintendent, his boss, had announced his retirement. Known as a talented leader and a gifted communicator, his boss was often referred to as the "great communicator" for his ability to connect with just about anyone.

The assistant superintendent started thinking about the possibility of interviewing to become superintendent, and the more he thought about it, the more excited he became. He had always been an optimist who wanted to fix the world. In his gut, he genuinely thought he could leverage the school system to change the trajectory of so many children and their families. In fact, he was reminded of a community presentation he had given at a local college. During that talk, he referenced Hart and Risley's study about the difference in the number of words children hear (including parent interactions and positive affirmations) depending on their social class.

They noted:

- The average number of words children hear per hour is 2,150 in professional families, 1,250 in working-class families, and 620 in poor families.
- By age four, a child from an advantaged, college-educated family hears forty-five million words, whereas a child from a low-income home hears only fifteen million. Differences in the length of time parents spend interacting with their children translate later into differences in vocabulary growth rate and achievement on IQ tests.
- By age four, children from professional homes hear seven hundred thousand positive affirmations from their parents, whereas a child from a low-income family hears about one hundred thousand.[2]

Hart and Risley concluded that children from more affluent backgrounds had more opportunities to develop a richer vocabulary, which would translate into higher achievement scores. As part of his talk, the assistant superintendent showed an example of his own school district's data at that time, which showed a huge gap in achievement.

At every grade level and at every school, children who participated in the National School Lunch Program (free/reduced lunch) underperformed their more affluent peers by nearly 30 percentage points. He commented that more than four out of every five African American students in his community participated in the federal lunch program. He looked around the auditorium and spoke some hard truths. The system was failing in a few ways. For one, its recruitment efforts had failed to create a genuine pipeline to diversify its teaching force. And although the school district had started having deeper conversations about equity, all the opportunities provided were exclusively voluntary.

He asked aloud:

Do we have honest conversations about who the children see when they are being taught? Do they see a reflection of themselves, meaning do they see someone who looks like them, who may have had a common experience? And do we continuously engage in self-reflection and honest dialogue around race, class, and gender issues?

The assistant superintendent came home and made the decision to apply for the superintendency.

In a letter he sent to the board of education, he stressed the urgency of continuity and how his experiences working in different environments, including his previous work in a metropolitan district, had prepared him to serve as the district's superintendent. The district, he observed, was rapidly changing, and it was seeing an increase in second-language learners (sixty-five different languages spoken) and families struggling with income and housing insecurities. He knew there wasn't enough time to fix everything. There's never enough time. What he proposed was to simplify what they were doing as a district and consider how they were using their time.

Let me pause for a moment in this leader's journey to becoming the district's next superintendent and ask you to consider the role of time in a school setting. The thing that always left me speechless about time is the percentage that a child *actually* spends in school and the amount of responsibility that communities and legislatures put on schools to fix nearly everything.

Fourteen percent.

That's it. That's the percentage of time that a child spends in school during a given year: 14 percent—8,760 hours in a year, of which children attend school 1,218 hours—that's 14 percent. And if you were to recalculate, deducting eight hours of sleep per day, then children are in school 21 percent of their waking hours. Schools, as Robert Putnam indicated in *Our Kids*,[3] cannot be responsible for everything. They are, however, a very good place to level the field and close opportunity gaps.

The assistant superintendent expressed in his letter to the board that he knew there were many possible levers to be pulled to improve student achievement. He chose a lever he believed to be true: improve access to improve outcomes. He followed up his letter to the board with a letter to principals in the district stressing that he valued the process and that the board would select the very best fit for the community. He had been fielding many emails from his colleagues, a challenge for any internal candidate for a position.

He knew that if he had the opportunity to interview for the job, he would need to develop a plan. He began sketching out a strategic plan that built on the school district's existing plan. For more than ten years, the school district operated an Achievement Gap Task Force, and he wanted to utilize the task force's conversations, adapting them into his own words and actions (and later into a scorecard so progress could be reported). It made sense, from his perspective, to highlight three areas of access, which he referred to as AEO:

- *Achievement* of all students as well as historically underperforming students.
- *Enrichment* access relating to higher-level career and technical education course enrollment, internships, and extracurricular activities.

- *Opportunity* gaps relating to attendance, discipline, graduation rates, and course participation (looking critically at who was taking advanced classes).

The superintendent selection process included applications and interviews, and when the assistant superintendent was named one of two finalists, he was invited to make a public presentation to the community. The board of education invited a former district superintendent to facilitate the process. Each candidate would be given time to present themselves and their vision for the school district. Each would then answer questions provided by the audience (which were curated by the former superintendent).

His speech focused on the areas of achievement, enrichment, and opportunity. He was looking for a way to highlight the three letters *AEO*. Just as these three vowels are the building blocks to unlocking written English, they were also the foundation for his vision. Access was his rallying cry, and he used AEO to call for:

- Access to a great curriculum.
- Access to skilled teachers and a nurturing environment.
- Access to experiences beyond the core curriculum.
- Access to interest-based activities before and after school.
- And access to school—a system that eliminated barriers for children.

He concluded by saying that AEO was a belief system that was more important today than ever before. He acknowledged that he wanted all the district's children to be able to access an excellent education and he declared himself committed to that. The board of education then chose its next superintendent during a closed session. It wasn't unanimous for either candidate. The assistant superintendent was selected on a 5–2 vote.

WHAT GOT OVERLOOKED?

Exploring what was overlooked is the first step in unpacking an experience. It requires a leader to serve as a lead learner and to be vulnerable. The leader took a step back and recognized that he had spent a great deal of time planning and politicking but had failed to sit down with current and retiring members of the superintendent's cabinet to ask them important questions such as:

- What would you say are/were your greatest accomplishments?
- What do you hope we will continue to prioritize?
- What perspectives should I consider as I begin to lead the school district?

Three simple questions would have shown a genuine desire to honor and value their contributions to the organization. Three simple questions would have helped the newly named superintendent to navigate the interview process relating to curriculum and instruction decisions as well as short- and long-range facility issues.

Instead, he had been so focused on winning over the board of education that he failed to attend to some of the internal stakeholders. That's the thing about the superintendency: you have to be aware of the internal and external dynamics of the system, which are both independent of but dependent on each other.

WHAT WAS LEARNED ABOUT RELATIONSHIPS?

As a candidate during the interview and selection process, the assistant superintendent was introduced to a political consultant. The two talked about his presentations. They worked on language to highlight his position as the internal candidate as a source of strength (for example, how consistency increases a community's trust in the district). Also, he was introduced to the idea that whipping up the votes meant he would need four votes to become superintendent.

They discussed each member of the board of education. There was an advantage to being the internal candidate. Three board members knew about his vision for the school district, supported consistency of leadership, and committed their support early. A fourth board member soon declared support. The question soon became whether the other three would show unity for the public and make the vote 7–0.

This would not be the case.

What was learned about relationships is that they can be transactional. One member wanted a commitment to support athletics. Another wanted to ensure that existing community partnerships would not be abandoned. More than anything, what was learned was that relationships can be incredibly emotional. Hurt feelings about past actions could interfere with one's ability to make a decision.

WHAT WAS FRUSTRATING?

The assistant superintendent knew that being the internal candidate also could be a liability. Often, school boards romanticize an unknown candidate as being superior in some way. Additionally, strong feelings about the departing superintendent can present a real challenge for an internal candidate. That happened in this case with one board member. She made it clear at the beginning of deliberations that she wouldn't vote for the assistant superintendent. She was angry that her son hadn't been hired as an administrator in the school district and blamed the outgoing superintendent and, by extension, the assistant superintendent, even though he had nothing to do with that job search.

The assistant superintendent also knew that another board member wouldn't vote for him because of his belief that the candidate was too inexperienced. The two talked briefly about it, and the candidate expressed his respect for that decision. After the selection process had concluded and he been selected, the newly appointed superintendent approached the board member and told him that he would make him proud. It was affirming that the board member took the superintendent aside a year later to tell him he was proud that he was the school district's superintendent.

Most frustrating for the candidate was one board member who didn't want to vote for him because of his determination to provide children access. She perceived AEO as a challenge to the status quo. In the end, four board members were committed to voting for him, which meant that one more "no" vote would have only weakened him as he assumed the role. She was convinced by others to vote for the candidate because a 5–2 vote looked a lot stronger than 4–3. That was incredibly frustrating. In retrospect, this likely played a role in how he initially led.

WHAT COULD HAVE BEEN DONE DIFFERENTLY?

When a candidate is selected to lead an organization, there is a transition from applicant to leader. At the end of the movie *The Candidate*, the newly elected senator, Robert Redford, seeks momentary refuge with his strategist, first in a service elevator and then in a hotel room. He's just won a hard-fought election to become a U.S. senator, and during the few seconds of solitude, his face, truly contemplative and obviously transformed, asks, "What do we do now?"

Superintendents feel this way when they've been named the CEO of their school district. In the case of the assistant superintendent, he was filled with jubilation. He had received many well wishes from inside the school district, from the community, and from leaders around the state. It was exhilarating to have such broad and seemingly genuine support. Everyone was counting on the district to succeed.

As he considered what was next, he launched into declarations of the district's *why*, *what*, and *how*. He described the *why*—getting to the district's purpose—as an almost insatiable itch. He returned to his original talking points and said the *why* would be three words: achievement, enrichment, and opportunity.

He stated that for many years, the district had been led by both an outstanding superintendent and a collaborative board of education. He said that they had cultivated confidence in their ability to be good stewards of taxpayer money. He said that they had established a ten-year facility plan and a five-year budget that maintained robust reserves and ensured a highly valuable bond rating.

He said that the administration, having been left a road map for facilities, would be able to focus primarily on academic achievement, enrichment offerings, and access to an excellent education for all students. He conceded that the road would be long and the work would be hard, but that it would be the most important work worth doing (borrowing a motivational quote by President Theodore Roosevelt).

He initially thought he was doing things right, painting a clear image of what was to come. Engaging in an after-action review, he realized what could have been done differently. He was pushing ahead with a clear focus, but he was doing so on his own. He had overlooked how essential it is to take a step back and understand the big picture.

Had he acknowledged that his previous role as the assistant superintendent gave him only a partial view of the school district, he would have been able to send a more thoughtful and inclusive message to other areas of the organization. He would have been able to show that he would take time to get to know those areas before making declarations about the system as a whole. This reminds me of a story.

A LESSON FROM *STAR TREK*

One Friday night, when the superintendent's children were younger, he chose to honor Leonard Nimoy's life by watching *Star Trek IV: The Voyage Home*. *Star Trek IV*, as some might recall, is the movie in which the crew of the *Enterprise* goes back in time to recover a humpback whale in order to save mankind. (In case you were thinking of renting it on a streaming service, don't. It's really long and outdated. To save you time, they rescue the whale and save mankind. You're welcome.)

However, halfway through the movie, his oldest son turned to him and said, "I really identify with Spock. He is logical and there is no ambiguity."

His middle son remarked, "Don't you wish you knew what whales were saying? I really wish I could talk to them."

And his youngest declared, "I never want to live on a ship where captains tell me what to do!"

Their responses captured their personalities perfectly. The story speaks to a similar realization by the newly named superintendent. He had overlooked his own narrow understanding of the system as a whole. He could have spent time with each department and school, listening to adults and children to better understand how each saw the world differently. He could have seen how their areas of responsibility were connected to other areas inside and outside the organization. It would have sent a powerful message and helped him to build enduring relationships because it would have shown that he valued people's roles in the organization.

WHAT WAS SOMETHING GOOD THAT CAME OUT OF THIS EXPERIENCE?

Often, the superintendent would think about *Sélavi*,[4] a Haitian story about a child named Sélavi, who, orphaned by war and alone in the world, ultimately finds a community of support. In that moment, when he realizes he is not alone, he is told, "Alone, we may be a single drop of water, but together we can be a mighty river. We must help each other to become strong!" That message is so powerful, and it stresses the importance of working as a team.

Following his appointment as superintendent, he was forced to make a midcourse correction. The feedback he had been receiving was not that of collaboration and compassion, but of hierarchy and authoritarianism. There's a difference between casting a vision as part of the selection process and serving as a leader once chosen. A leader harvests the collective wisdom of the organization. A leader ensures that his or her vision aligns well inside and outside the organization. The new superintendent made a critical adjustment.

He scheduled a meeting with every assistant principal, principal, coordinator, and director—more than 125 conversations over many months. He expressed a desire to know about their professional paths, their goals, and areas where they wanted support. Of the educators he met, he asked three questions:

- What kind of learning environment do we want for children?
- What kind of learner do we want to cultivate?
- What type of learning do we want for children?

Those conversations represented the most meaningful investment of time. He got to know the leaders of the schools, and he looked for ways to support their goals. He became aware of formal and informal nested patterns, the written norms versus the unwritten ones. He continued to make such meetings an important part of onboarding new leaders to the school district. In subsequent years, in addition to meeting them and learning about their goals, he took the opportunity to share the district's values and its major initiatives. In time, he learned to better share the leadership in designing the district's direction.

WATERS CENTER FOR SYSTEMS THINKING HABIT

A Leader Seeks to Understand the Big Picture

Think back to when you assumed the responsibility of guiding the work in your organization. How did you maintain balance between the big picture and important details? What steps did you take to understand the system's formal and informal nested patterns?

NOTES

1. Roger A. Gafke, *A History of Public Education in Columbia* (Columbia, MO: Public School District, 1978), 89–91.

2. Betty Hart and Todd R. Risley, *Meaningful Differences in the Everyday Experience of Young American Children* (Baltimore: Brookes, 1995).

3. Robert D. Putnam, *Our Kids: The American Dream in Crisis* (New York: Simon & Schuster, 2016), 163.

4. Youme Landowne, *Sélavi, That Is Life* (El Paso, TX: Cinco Puntos Press, 2005).

Chapter 3

A New Leader, an
Antiquated System

Growth is painful. Change is painful. But nothing is as painful as staying stuck somewhere you don't belong.

—N. R. Narayana Murthy

What happened?
The communication of a district's purpose, values, and goals.
What got overlooked?
When a leader relies on an oral presentation just weeks before the start of the school year, confusion, anxiety, and false starts can be expected.
What was learned about relationships?
When a leader is building trust in a vision, relationships are imperative.
What was frustrating?
Although an attempt was made to lay out a clear plan, it was not necessarily well received.
What could have been done differently?
A collective vision should have been established before discussions about accountability.
What was something good that came out of this experience?
A lead learner takes a step back, makes a midcourse correction, and finds opportunities to share a vision for the organization.

It is common for principals to do home visits. Offering to meet in a place other than the school building or district office can demonstrate respect for the fact that these locations can raise one's stress level. Homes visits do so much more. You get to see family photos, their prized portraits and family celebrations memorialized. When leaders visit homes, it usually means that problems need solving or fences need mending. Some superintendents continue to do home visits because it keeps them connected to their district's families.

During one such visit, the superintendent met a grandmother who was so proud of her three-year-old grandson. He was seated in a dark room, his legs crossed, and his eyes fixed on the television screen. She said, "He's learning so much by watching these shows." The superintendent knew that his place, especially in her space, was not to contradict the grandmother. Instead, he left that visit with a desire to find ways to facilitate a community conversation about school readiness and early childhood learning. He decided he would host a world café.

World cafés[1] create an opportunity for people to come together to harvest the collective wisdom of the community. They include a brief presentation followed by a specific question and a lot of uninterrupted time for small groups to talk and listen.

The superintendent hosted his first world café at the community recreation center because he wanted a location with easy access to public transportation. On this night, he welcomed everyone in attendance and told them about his recent experience visiting the home of the child watching a children's television program as a substitute for school. He did this to highlight that all parents want the very best for their children and that they make decisions thinking that they are helping them.

He then shared some of the school district's kindergarten skills assessment data, an assessment given three times a year to monitor a child's progress in literacy skills. Children with access to high-quality early childhood learning experiences entered kindergarten with many more skills. He noted the difference in the disaggregated data, with twice as many affluent children scoring above benchmark as compared to their peers participating in the National School Lunch Program.

He said, "The school district has a goal that all children will graduate with the necessary skills to enter a college and/or career program of their choice. If that is to happen, we need to look at how our children enter school. We need to work with our community to make sure children enter school ready to succeed."

At this point, the participants were asked to give the school district their best thinking on ways to support children. The superintendent said, "During this session, we will be asking you to share your definition of readiness as well as your experiences with preparing children for social/emotional and academic success." Each table had a facilitator who was responsible for ensuring that everyone was heard and that all voices were respected. There were placemats on every table for participants to write down ideas, ask questions, and respond to other participants.

Following the world café, the superintendent made a presentation to the board of education. The three themes that emerged as a result of the world café were healthy children, access to education, and access to support. The superintendent decided that entering school ready to learn had to be one of the school district's goals. He continued to make early learning a focus throughout his superintendency.

The district built an early learning center to increase the number of preschool classrooms to twenty-six. The building also housed the early childhood special education program as well as parent educators who worked with families in their homes. During his last year as superintendent, the program was awarded the state's early childhood program of the year. He was proud of the early learning programs and felt the world café gave him the permission to expand and deliver on the community's feedback. The world café can make a superintendent feel like they have a mandate. A lesson he would need to learn was to make sure his team felt similarly.

BUILDING A TEAM

At some point, all superintendents have to build a leadership team. Sometimes it's right after they've been hired. Other times, it's a result of someone leaving. This superintendent was new to the position, and he needed to find a replacement assistant superintendent.

Most leaders consider the first year as the most important. They want to project confidence and compassion. They want to take time to listen and demonstrate an ability to make decisions, especially in education, when they're repeatedly told, "This is the *only* time this group of third graders will be third graders."

In a district-wide letter, the superintendent said he would spend a few weeks working on hiring and that he would continue to send out communications to highlight progress and next steps. He said that once he had assembled a new team, he'd begin working on what the district priorities would be. He said they would need to work on the priorities for each individual school, stating that he had a plan for that. And then he thanked them for listening and for their relentless commitment to the children and to their colleagues in the district.

A TALE OF TWO DISTRICTS

Have you ever seen the video of the two children, both starting kindergarten, but already experiencing a gap even before instruction ever takes place?[2] Having different experiences before a child even enters school (and every year thereafter) shows the importance of uninterrupted learning for children. It is a reminder that children come to school from different circumstances.

If you were to liken it to a baseball game, some students come to school already on third base (ninety feet from home plate), while others stand at the plate, maybe with a helmet and bat, and sometimes not. The video highlights the vastly different experiences of a community's children. For the superintendent intent on prioritizing early learning and committed to establishing goals for the district, this video highlighted the two districts he would be leading.

What this video also shows is that children who may have started at a disadvantage cannot be satisfied with typical progress over a ten-month period. For the superintendent, it meant that learning had to be accelerated. He felt it would take a clear vision and the design of better systems to do that.

At one of his first official board meetings, he told the board of education that, as an institution in the industry of education, he wanted their district to be the best district. He said he wanted their school district to be managed and regarded by its peers as the best. He declared that would be their vision. Their mission—what the organization did—would be something different.

"We exist," he said, "because we want to provide an excellent education for all students." He defined an excellent education to mean that all children would enter school ready to learn and that all students would be reading on grade level by the end of third grade. He said this would mean that all children would make smooth transitions into and out of middle school and that all children would graduate and enter a two-year, four-year, or career program. "An excellent education," he said. "That's why we exist."

In the spring before officially becoming superintendent, he visited a local company, a two-time Malcolm Baldridge National Quality Award recipient. He wanted to learn about its systems, specifically how the company monitored progress and defined its vision, mission, purpose, and values. At that same meeting with the board of education, he announced the purpose statement of the district: "We provide an asset to our community by preparing children for an ever-changing and unpredictable future."

He then announced their core values, those nonnegotiable values that would guide them. It would be these values, he said, that they would recruit for. It would be these values that would govern their decisions to retain employees. The values would be: honesty, transparency, a focus on what works, mutual respect, persistence, teamwork, a positive approach, adaptability, and commitment.

Finally, he shared eight organizational goals. These goals would be tied to state accountability systems and their locally prioritized measures. They were:

1. We will be fiscally responsible with taxpayer money.
2. We will partner with the community to help children enter school ready to succeed.
3. Students will read on level by the end of third grade.
4. We will actively support student transitions.
5. Students will graduate with the necessary skills to enroll in college and/or a career program of their choice.
6. Ninety percent of students will attend school at least 90 percent of the time.
7. Out-of-school suspension numbers will decrease for all student groups.
8. Students will demonstrate academic progress as measured by state accountability systems.

He told the board of education that the district would monitor these goals with a scorecard and create a support system for schools that were eligible for additional assistance. He told them that they would share their goals widely so that they would serve as a rallying cry for the whole community.

WHAT GOT OVERLOOKED?

You've read what happened and you are no doubt already thinking about the many things this superintendent overlooked. Did he even bring the goals to his administrative team before bringing them to the board of education? Yes, he did.

He made a presentation to the entire administration in August. Every principal, assistant principal, director, and coordinator assembled at a middle school, and he presented all of this to them orally. He didn't have a PowerPoint presentation or handouts. When asked why he didn't think to give his leaders something tangible to leave with, he couldn't explain why he made that decision. "It's possible," he said, "that I wanted to impress them with my ability to give a presentation without notes." And then he laughed at himself for how silly that sounded.

Without a presentation or handouts, there was little chance that they would have processed everything he said and an even smaller chance that they'd share the information with their own faculties and departments. Additionally, by presenting to them in August, he had missed an opportunity to influence their summer planning. Instead of aligning district and building goals, he had to rely on the hope that they'd match up. Hope is not a strategy. This is like attempting to build a bridge from opposite sides that connects perfectly in the middle.

Second, without harvesting the collective wisdom of the organization, without enacting a process wherein internal and external stakeholders could offer their insights, he identified eight goals by himself. One of his board members privately told him, "You know, when you're focused on eight things, you're really focused on nothing." The superintendent remembered bristling. "Which goal should we remove?" he asked. That wasn't the board member's point, and it would take time before the superintendent came to understand his counsel and make the necessary midcourse correction.

WHAT WAS LEARNED ABOUT RELATIONSHIPS?

A few years ago, Todd Rose, a Harvard professor, gave a talk about individualizing education for children. He asked the audience if they were aware of the 1960s Stanford University marshmallow experiment. In short, researchers put a marshmallow in front of a toddler. They then told the child that if the child could wait a few minutes to eat the marshmallow, he or she would get a second marshmallow. The researchers left the room and filmed the child as he or she waited. Some children could wait a long time, and others simply ate the marshmallow right away. The researchers then extrapolated that a child who could wait longer to eat the marshmallow would experience success later in life.[3]

The study is interesting but has been debunked on some level recently because it ignores context.[4] A child living in poverty might have a very different relationship to the traditional marshmallow study. She might simply eat it! Context matters. A new study was done, and this time the researchers replicated the protocols, but the participating adults (i.e., the researchers promising the additional marshmallow) were either a trusted person or someone the children didn't know (they had done an exercise to build or erode trust). In the rooms where the trusted adult promised to bring back an additional marshmallow, the children waited. In rooms where the adult was not known, the children didn't wait. Relationships make a difference.

In every school, our teachers and staff work incredibly hard to build meaningful relationships with children. It's those relationships that make all the difference in whether or not children feel like they belong. When the superintendent made presentations about eight organizational goals, context mattered, especially among those with whom he had an established relationship.

When he presented the information internally, he discovered teachers and leaders felt overwhelmed by the enormity of the job that they would have to do. Publicly, however, he found a much more receptive audience. He had been actively building relationships in many civic groups, which appreciated the level of transparency. Wherever he went, he was asked what these groups could do to help the district succeed. It was a paradox the superintendent hadn't anticipated, and he hadn't realized it quickly. He found strong alliances being built with community partners and some distancing from educators. The superintendent had to learn to build relationships throughout the organization before he could expect anyone to subscribe to his vision.

WHAT WAS FRUSTRATING?

In public education, there is a lot of finger-pointing. Legislators point fingers at public education and promote reforms like vouchers. Parents accuse schools of teaching to the middle and not challenging their high-achieving child or intervening with their struggling child. So when the superintendent announced the eight district goals and published a scorecard to track progress, he was frustrated by the lack of enthusiasm for what he thought was a clear plan.

When he visited every building and department, he used the metaphor of an aircraft carrier. He said, "Just like everyone on an aircraft carrier rallies around the pilots, we will rally around our teachers and prioritize their mission to provide children with an excellent education." The response was tepid at best. The absence of buy-in was frustrating.

WHAT COULD HAVE BEEN DONE DIFFERENTLY?

When leaders focus on the good things happening, they can take an appreciative approach to continuous improvement. They look at what is going well and seek additional ways to celebrate success. When asked what the superintendent could have done differently in this situation, he recognized how his focus on process deprived him of the opportunity to build enduring relationships.

The scorecard presentations caused anxiety for school faculties. They were interpreted as "tracking" schools. They caused confusion. The superintendent hadn't talked about celebrating their efforts, and they had not seen his presentation in August. They simply were presented with a scorecard.

What could have been done differently? The superintendent could have first spent time introducing himself to the school district. He could have shared his experiences, his personal values, and his moral focus before launching into the goals and its companion scorecard. The superintendent recognized that he was so incredibly ambitious and motivated to get started that he forgot to follow a human-centered approach. He could have mapped out the year and done a better job of sharing the vision and goals in a way that was less overwhelming. He could have enlisted the support of school administrators so that the message was not delivered by only the superintendent, but was instead a shared message. He could have put people first.

WHAT WAS SOMETHING GOOD THAT CAME OUT OF THIS EXPERIENCE?

Launching one's vision is one of the more difficult challenges for any leader. Building consensus among different perspectives, values, and experiences is not easy. People are willing to bend in a new direction once their values are identified and given credence. So how do you become the high-achieving school district that everyone genuinely wants to become? You create opportunities for high levels of collaboration and make sure it is a nested pattern.

The superintendent in this scenario identified some bright spots to his school faculty visits. He recognized that he had presented a system design inconsistent with how the district had operated previously. He was proposing to centralize a system that had been decentralized for decades. The individual departments and schools had operated independently of each other. They often didn't know what was happening throughout the system. He was determined to change that.

He began spending time harvesting the wisdom of the organization by asking teacher advisories and staff leadership teams the three questions he had asked leaders:

- What kind of learner do we want to cultivate?
- What type of learning do we want for children?
- What kind of learning environment do we want for children?

He continued meeting one-on-one with district leaders. He continued to get to know them better. He reframed the conversation and reframed the metaphor. Instead of an aircraft carrier, he conjured the image of a mosaic (one picture made with many pieces) to highlight that although they were one school district, they were special because of the people in the district. He walked each leader through the scorecard and took the time to answer questions. He showed how the state's evaluation model would be embedded into their plan so that they wouldn't be jumping from one plan to another.

Finally, he shared how the board of education would be evaluating him. They would be looking for progress in providing effective instructional programs, managing resources, and responding to community interests and needs. He felt that by being vulnerable with how he was being evaluated, they would see how all the pieces would go together, like a mosaic.

WATERS CENTER FOR SYSTEMS THINKING HABIT

A Leader Considers How a System's Structure Generates Its Behavior

The superintendent realized that the organization had been decentralized in many ways, independent and isolated. The system was being asked to make a significant adjustment.

Think about your organization and the interaction of the parts. How does your organization and the interaction of its parts create the behavior that emerges? What parts work collaboratively? Which ones need extra attention and support?

NOTES

1. Juanita Brown and David Isaacs, *The World Café: Shaping Our Futures through Conversations That Matter* (San Francisco: Berrett-Koehler, 2006).
2. National Summer Learning Association, "NBC's Brian Williams on Summer Learning Loss," YouTube, www.youtube.com/watch?v=M2haD7FhMys (accessed October 23, 2022).
3. Walter Mischel and Ebbe B. Ebbesen, "Attention in Delay of Gratification," *Journal of Personality and Social Psychology* 16, no. 2 (1970): 329–37.
4. Patricia Kasak Saxler, "The Marshmallow Test: Delay of Gratification and Independent Rule Compliance" (PhD diss., Harvard Graduate School of Education, 2016).

Chapter 4

The Truth about Their Data

There comes a point where we need to stop just pulling people out of the river. We need to go upstream and find out why they're falling in.

—Desmond Tutu

What happened?
An idealistic pragmatist tells the whole truth.
What got overlooked?
The superintendent should have taken the time to engage his team.
What was learned about relationships?
Fleeting relationships are like buildings constructed on sand. They lack stability.
What was frustrating?
Practicing vulnerability is seen as a weakness.
What could have been done differently?
Harvesting the collective wisdom of the organization leads to collaborative decisions.
What was something good that came out of this experience?
The greatest learning happens when leaders serve as lead learners and confront their mistakes.

In the Jewish faith, a bar mitzvah recognizes when a boy becomes a man. During the ceremony of a bar mitzvah, something beautiful occurs. The rabbi calls the soon-to-be man to the front of the congregation. He invites the boy's parents and grandparents to join him. They stand in a line and face the congregation. And at that moment, the rabbi brings forth the Torah and hands it to the grandparents. They then turn to the parents and hand the Torah to them, who then carefully hand the Torah to their son. As this is happening, the rabbi recites the words *l'dor vador*, which translates to "from generation to generation."

This part of the service is incredibly moving and tremendously symbolic. First of all, the three generations standing together and being reminded of their connection to each other is beautiful. Second, the actual act of passing the Torah is poignant as well. The Torah is really heavy. And so is the responsibility of carrying the expectations of the many generations that have come before you. The sacrifices and successes of those who came before you should be a focal point, particularly during this moment of joy and celebration.

Through life events such as these—a first communion for Catholics or the *arangetram* for Indian families, for example—leaders can tell stories of their school district. It gives them an opportunity to connect with their community. They invariably speak of the generations who came before them and the decisions they made so that they'd be where they are now. Superintendents use these rites of passage to speak of the decisions still needed to be made so that future generations will look back and give thanks for the investment in their future. When a community votes for a tax increase, for example, it is a *l'dor vador* decision. Public education is in a *l'dor vador* moment right now. Decisions made today will have ramifications well into the future.

Peter Senge, author of *The Fifth Discipline*, is an influence on the model for human-centered school transformation. His work on systems thinking and his affiliation with the Waters Center have certainly influenced the way I think about leadership. He has described himself as an idealistic pragmatist, which is the perfect way to talk about this chapter and the superintendent's experiences.

NAVIGATING DISCUSSIONS OF RACE AND CLASS

In 2015, the University of Missouri received national attention when protests about racial justice erupted on its Columbia campus. Both the university president and chancellor resigned from their positions, and school districts across the state began developing or strengthening their equity programs.

The events on the university campus—and in the community (the head of the local police officers association sent a Christmas card showing a car on fire in Ferguson, Missouri, and his handwritten message said, "Only 7 more looting days 'til Christmas!")—became a turning point for the equity work for the school district, from discussions about socioeconomics (class) to an emphasis on race. But it wasn't immediate.

Six years later, after district-run professional training on the history of Black Lives Matter (including discussions on how to respond to comments like "well, I think *all* lives matter"), the county's emergency management center advised the district's safety and security director of the following 9-1-1 call:

DISPATCHER: 9-1-1. How can I help you?

CALLER: I am calling because I want this stopped.

DISPATCHER: This is 9-1-1. Is there an emergency?

CALLER: Yes, my wife was forced to attend a training . . . an equity training, and she was told to feel guilty for being White.

DISPATCHER: I am sorry sir, but this is 9-1-1.

CALLER: I know it's 9-1-1. This is an emergency.

DISPATCHER: When did this happen, sir?

CALLER: Yesterday.

DISPATCHER: Yesterday?

CALLER: Yes, my wife went to a district training yesterday and learned about Black Lives Matter.

DISPATCHER: Sir, this is 9-1-1. This number is for calling in emergencies. Goodbye.

FOCUS OF RACE

Conversations about race are some of the most difficult for educators. Yet they are necessary for school districts to initiate and sustain. There are the internal perspectives of students and staff, as well as parents and the community at large, not to mention the added challenge of when one's community is in close proximity to a state capital, which attracts the attention of politicians and political operatives. The superintendent in this book experienced this firsthand.

WHAT IS THE ENTRY POINT FOR LARGE-SCALE TRAININGS ON EQUITY?

In 2015, superintendents across the nation were looking to expand their equity efforts. The superintendent's school district had taken a significant step forward through its relationship with the National Conference for Community and Justice of Metropolitan St. Louis, an organization whose stated mission is "to promote inclusion for all people."[1] The district decided to add eight district trainers annually to its equity team in order to represent a range of identities and to be available to support the school district's effort to improve outcomes.

The superintendent initially thought the entry point to discussions about equity would be better approached through discussions of poverty, *not* through race. Michael Brown's death in Ferguson sparked protests throughout the state, the NAACP led a statewide march to the state capital, and the school district was looking toward April, when it would be asking a divided community to approve a substantial tax increase.

The superintendent recalled that the district's equity team was disappointed by his decision to focus on poverty. He explained that the way he reached this decision by using the metaphor of a house. The house represented equity and had two entrances. He said, "We all want to get inside that house. The question is how." One way was a really, *really* sticky door (race) and the other less so (poverty). He reasoned that if the district could rally people to consider the needs of children in poverty, it would be able to address race as well.

For the entire year, the school district engaged in trainings about poverty. The superintendent showed them that children born into poverty in their county were only 17 percent more likely to escape from poverty than other counties in America.[2] He invited experts to conduct school visits and to facilitate trainings on how poverty affects the brain.

The district's equity team led entire faculties in a "poverty module" to simulate the excruciating decisions families make and the enduring consequences of generational poverty. When one learns that it is not uncommon for a family in poverty to use their child's social security number to access utilities, it is heartbreaking. The work was good and important. However, the district's data told them that they had to look more closely at the other door of this metaphorical house.

The superintendent decided to bring together every teacher in the school district for one-hour sessions in a high school gymnasium. He said, "I can stand in front of every Rotary Club and say that third graders in Columbia read on a fourth-grade level. But the moment we disaggregate the data between African American children and their White peers, we see something incredibly alarming."

He showed them that in third grade, African American children read below the third-grade level while their White peers read at the fourth-grade level. He showed them how this problem persisted in later years as well. As eighth graders, African American children read on a sixth-grade level while their White peers read on a ninth-grade level. Additionally, in a comparison of fourteen categories of achievement on state assessments, African American students from all over the state of Missouri outperformed the district's African American students. It wasn't just economics. The school district was failing its African American students. They had to look critically at their systems, practices, and beliefs.

The superintendent was confident he'd get buy-in right from the start. After all, they had done good work around poverty. Now, he reasoned, they'd work together to tackle the issue of the achievement gap. If anyone could do it, they could.

Right before the school year, the superintendent presented his district's reading and math data to three African American superintendents from urban and suburban districts. He distinctly remembered saying to them at the moment he revealed the more than three-year gap in reading by ninth grade, "And this is where the room gets quiet." Their feedback was a genuine but cautious "good luck." They knew he'd face resistance.

The school district has come a long way since those 2015 conversations. With that said, an after-action review gives the superintendent the ability to look back to see what went well and what could have been different.

WHAT GOT OVERLOOKED?

Leaders are constantly barraged with problems that need solutions. Experience has taught me that leaders don't often have time to pause, take a step back, and distinguish between the terms *emergency* and *emergent*. When leaders approach everything as an emergency, they exhaust the system. In fact, the system can no longer distinguish what is an actual emergency because everything, it seems, has become one. When adjusting practices, leaders must allow time to introduce concepts. They must allow time to shift perspectives. A growth mindset is not a switch you turn on and off.

In the case of the academic underperformance that he had revealed to the organization, the superintendent treated the situation as an emergency and not as an emergent issue. Deciding to begin talking about race instead of class was a decisive action. However, he didn't take the time to use his team effectively. He overlooked their ability to help lead the work.

WHAT WAS LEARNED ABOUT RELATIONSHIPS?

When asked what he learned about relationships, the superintendent said that he learned they can be deceptive. Throughout his time as a principal and then as district leader, he had built a strong relationship with an activist in his community. The partnership was built on a common compelling purpose. He assumed this person would rally behind them and say, "Finally! You're talking about race, class, sex, sexual orientation, religion, and ability. It's difficult work. It's important work. And you're doing it." Instead, he was disappointed to find himself defending their equity work. At one point, there were even public calls for people's resignations.

It was a hard lesson to learn. It didn't stop him from working to build relationships with others who sought to understand their goals. In fact, he described how several positive partnerships developed, and how those individuals, who were once outspoken critics, met with his team, and they worked together. It was through this experience, he noted, that he was reminded that sharing leadership builds trust and creates enduring relationships.

WHAT WAS FRUSTRATING?

The most frustrating part of this situation was the reaction by some about how the district was reporting the data. The superintendent knew he could stand in front of any group and say their third graders were performing above grade level. He also knew the district would never achieve its moral focus without first being honest about where it was falling short.

However, in declaring this honesty, the school district, specifically the superintendent, was accused of spotlighting African American children. He was accused of blaming them. Yet he was doing what every leader should do: he was leading with vulnerability and saying, "We have work to do in this specific area."

Internally, pockets of leaders and teachers felt the superintendent was blaming them for the underachievement of children. If it is generally understood that a system does exactly what it was designed to do, then looking inward would be essential in this situation. The superintendent was frustrated by what appeared to be an unwillingness to step back and ask how the system could be designed differently.

WHAT COULD HAVE DONE BEEN DIFFERENTLY?

Looking back, the superintendent realized he wasn't leading the way he had been taught to lead. The human-centered school transformation model has three trailheads leading to a culture of deeper learning. One of them is leaders' learning work.[3]

Specifically, he hadn't harvested the collective wisdom of the people most impacted by the decisions. He hadn't served as a lead learner. He failed to admit he had made a mistake by making decisions with little input. More than anything, he hadn't applied systems and design thinking. For example, he didn't ask, as the Waters Center for Systems Thinking aptly puts it, "How much time do we need to allow for consideration of this issue and how can we manage the tension that exists when issues are not resolved immediately?"[4]

WHAT WAS SOMETHING GOOD THAT CAME OUT OF THIS EXPERIENCE?

Leaders know their greatest learning happens when they serve as lead learners and confront their mistakes. When that happens, innovations and promising practices emerge. After a midcourse correction, this is what happened:

- The school district established a pipeline for locally educated, culturally competent students to receive full scholarships (including room, board, and books) to become teachers in their school district.
- The district supported student-led organizations as they became more involved in equity in the school district and the community.
- The district created a chief equity officer role, a cabinet position, to lead the equity work and influence policy and practices.
- The superintendent became a member of the district's equity team as well. The team expanded its work beyond faculty meetings and took it to all new teachers. The superintendent trained this group so that his actions would align with his words.
- The entire board of education actively participated in multiple equity trainings. This required them to be willing to be vulnerable in a public space with regular media coverage.
- The school district designed a robust multitiered system of support and aligned its budget to meet the needs of the district's children.

All leaders are tasked with leading their organizations to shift beliefs and practices. They are all trying to figure out how to bridge the gaps that exist. In this case, academically, the school district wasn't seeing the results it had hoped for. It needed to look at its systems, practices, and perceptions about children. If it didn't try to approach the work in *some* way, whether it be race or class, it would fail.

So maybe the answer didn't lie in where to start, because everyone will not universally agree which course of action is right. Instead, the answer was to genuinely include all the individuals who would make this work possible. Work together.

In the end, notwithstanding the outrageous calls to 9-1-1, the disturbing e-mails and offensive letters, and the phone calls and public comments during school board meetings, the work this school district started was extremely important. The superintendent learned the power of shared leadership, of leading with vulnerability, and of collaborative systems.

Most of all, he learned how powerful an after-action review process can be for an individual leader and his or her entire team.

WATERS CENTER FOR SYSTEMS THINKING HABIT

A Leader Considers the Impact of Time Delays When Exploring Cause-and-Effect Relationships

Think about a decision you've made in your personal or professional life. How did you handle the tension between your actions and the results you had expected to see?

Now think about a decision you're about to make in your personal or professional life. What will that decision look like right after you act? What will it look like a week from now? A month from now? A year from now?

NOTES

1. "FaciliTrainer Certification Program (FTCP)," NCCJ-St. Louis, www.nccjstl.org /ftcp (accessed October 23, 2022).

2. "The Best and Worst Places to Grow Up: How Your Area Compares," *New York Times*, May 4, 2015, www.nytimes.com/interactive/2015/05/03/upshot/the-best -and-worst-places-to-grow-up-how-your-area-compares.html (accessed October 22, 2022).

3. "Our Approach," Transformational Leadership Initiative, https://cpb-us-w2 .wpmucdn.com/sites.wustl.edu/dist/7/2590/files/2018/05/twoPager_021618-153jco2 .pdf (accessed October 23, 2022).

4. "Habits of a Systems Thinker," Thinking Tools Studio, https://thinkingtoolsstudio .waterscenterst.org/cards (accessed October 23, 2022).

Chapter 5

The Year They All Left

The worst is not so long as we can say "This is the worst."

—Edgar, *King Lear* (act 4, scene 1)

What happened?
Eighty percent of the superintendent's cabinet retired or resigned.
What got overlooked?
A focus on the district's mission should be a collaborative process, not the product of a single perspective.
What was learned about relationships?
Successful leaders balance relationships and systems.
What was frustrating?
Change takes time, but leaders are not given time.
What could have been done differently?
A shared image of success would have created a clearer path.
What was something good that came out of this experience?
Creativity and courage (innovations) are achievable when processes are clear.

One morning, the superintendent walked into the board office and noticed a child no more than seven years old sitting with two women. He walked over, introduced himself, and asked the child if he would like to give him a high five. The child didn't respond. He just looked at him with a polite but cautious face. Almost immediately, one of the two women introduced herself as the family's translator. The other woman and the child were refugees from the Democratic Republic of Congo.

Very quickly the superintendent learned that the other woman was not the child's mother, but an aunt. In fact, the translator explained, she was not his aunt by relation, but through circumstance. She raised him as her own child after he had witnessed the murders of his parents. The "aunt" knew a lot about this type of trauma. She had lost her family to violence, too. The translator went on to tell the superintendent how the child checked every window and every door, every evening, just to make sure they were safe.

The superintendent would think of this story whenever he experienced something uncomfortable or inconvenient. It was a story that also motivated him when he considered the kind of leader he wanted to be. In the previous chapter, the term *l'dor vador*—from generation to generation—was introduced. The superintendent wanted his decisions to reflect the deliberation with which he and his team were trying to set the stage for future generations. It was always his hope that future generations would look back with appreciation for everything his team had done to position them for success.

Many years before, the superintendent wrote a personal reflection. He had just finished reading *Letters to a Young Chef* by Daniel Boulud. He and his family had recently moved for his wife's career, and the superintendent was working to finish his doctorate. He spent a lot of time translating interviews he had conducted from Spanish to English and cooking. His wife, pregnant with their second child at the time, endured multicourse meals when all she really wanted was a grilled cheese sandwich.

As he read Chef Boulud's book, the superintendent copied down, word for word, what he had written about building a team. The advice spurred a connection because even though it was a book about the restaurant industry, it was a book about leadership. Boulud wrote:

> If you become a top chef, being good is not good enough. You need to hire great. . . . If you always work with good, dedicated people, both above and below you, then you will learn to thrive in an environment of excellence.[1]

The superintendent, who by now was entering his third year, would look back on this quote and note how it almost seemed to foreshadow the year ahead. The third year is a pivotal year for superintendents. In this case, the superintendent would be navigating the most difficult year of his career, politically. He would remark that even the global pandemic a few years later wasn't as professionally difficult as his third year.

You know how sometimes a television show has an episode that serves as a retrospective, where it tells you what happened by going back days, weeks, or months to show how it got to a particular point? Some people complain about these episodes because they prefer to see how a story unfolds chronologically, but in the following example, a retrospective makes sense.

At the end of this superintendent's third year, 80 percent of his cabinet had left. Some left because they had planned to retire. Others left because they said they had found a dream job in the state they had departed just a year before. He perceived one left because they didn't have a compatible leadership style.

Additionally, the superintendent was trying to make sense of a lawsuit against the school district filed by a district administrator over leadership position they didn't get. This led to another lawsuit by another administrator, which only exacerbated the existing tension.

The superintendent's cabinet needed to be a healthy team when they were what Patrick Lencioni refers to as a smart team.[2] The team lacked cohesion, trust, and the ability to be both smart and compassionate. At the end of the school year, the cabinet dissolved, and the principal was forced to start again. While he was rebuilding his team, a member of the board of education insisted on conducting exit interviews with departing cabinet members. The superintendent described this as a painful experience, but one in which he learned a lot about systems, relationships, and leadership.

Now you know what happened at the end of the superintendent's third year. Let's return to the beginning of the year to experience how the superintendent got there and reflect on what he learned.

FROM THE BEGINNING

The superintendent was in his third year as superintendent. He had enrolled in the American Association of School Administrator's National Superintendent Certification Program and was finally beginning to understand the relationship of the superintendent and the board of education more deeply. In a journal entry the summer before the school year began, he listed the areas for major work during the coming year:

- central office culture
- student attendance
- out-of-school suspensions
- student achievement

CENTRAL OFFICE CULTURE

Superintendents must partner with the board of education. When they fail to do that, they risk alienating the very people who hired them. This superintendent realized he hadn't fully learned how to be a partner with the board of education. If someone were to ask him how he was treating the board until this point, he would have said he was tolerating them. He took their phone calls, met with them at the agenda-setting meetings, and attended their regular meetings. It wasn't until he met the director of the National School Board Association that it became clear how essential the relationship between a school board and its superintendent was.

His presentation led the superintendent to this quote: "A strong board and superintendent partnership does not develop by chance. Such a partnership is grounded in the superintendent's respect for the opinions of each individual board member and communicating with each one regarding their interests and goals for the district."[3]

The board members are elected by the community. They represent the community's interests. Genuine respect for their positions and perspectives was something that he had initially overlooked.

ATTENDANCE

The school district maintained a publicly available scorecard of a number of metrics. Aligned to his state's accountability measures, his district set a goal of children attending school 90 percent of the time. Nearly 90 percent of the district's elementary school students attended school 90 percent of the time. Middle school and high school students were a different story. Its juniors and seniors were the most alarming. Nearly one in every four juniors and seniors had missed more than seventeen days of school.

The superintendent was determined to find new ways to improve attendance because the traditional approaches were not working. Calls home and conferences with the students were not having the effect that he had hoped for. Plus, suspending kids for not coming to school is counterintuitive, keeping them out of school even more (the district did rewrite its policy to prohibit this).

OUT-OF-SCHOOL SUSPENSIONS

When leaders look at suspensions, school districts consider the overall numbers of students being suspended. They also look to see if the ratio of suspensions is disproportionate. For example, if African American students make up 25 percent of your enrollment, then it is reasonable to expect the overall percentage of suspensions for this group of students to be 25 percent. If the percentage of suspensions for this group is 55 percent, for instance, then your suspension data is disproportionate. African American students make up a greater percentage of suspensions than any other group.

That was the case for this district. Suspensions were disproportionate. Also troubling were the reasons why students were being suspended. Terms like "disrespect" and "defiance" appeared more often on referrals for African American students than children of other races. Although suspension numbers were trending in a better direction overall (fewer students were being suspended), they remained disproportionate.

STUDENT ACHIEVEMENT

One thing school leaders discover quickly is that students cannot learn if they are not in school. Student achievement and out-of-school suspensions go hand in hand. If children are suspended, they can't access school, which puts them further behind. The superintendent saw achievement gaps and wanted the district's intervention systems to target the skills that students needed in order to be successful.

These three areas: attendance, suspensions, and student achievement helped the superintendent to narrow the district's focus to three goals. He adopted this rallying cry:

- Get them to school (attendance).
- Keep them in class (suspensions).
- Catch them up and accelerate their learning (student achievement).

The superintendent worked closely with district leaders, the board of education, and community members to craft a strategic plan that incorporated this rallying cry. They crafted a shared image of what it would look like for all children to graduate from high school college ready, career ready, and ready for life. That image included multiple pathways. In order to accomplish this plan, they agreed that they needed to see new approaches to improve attendance, discipline, and systems of academic support. Looking back, the superintendent remarked how that was some of the most rewarding work.

WHAT GOT OVERLOOKED?

Many years ago, I wrote my dissertation on why students in a complex system learn or don't learn English. Parents were led to make decisions that didn't align well with what second language acquisition researchers knew to be true about learning a new language. One conclusion I reached was that the system lacked clear direction and was unintentionally harming children. I can remember struggling with the role of researcher and that of practitioner.[4] The

struggle to keep those two roles separate is hard when it might mean witness-
ing the consequences of well-intentioned but ultimately poorly informed
decision makers.

Similarly for this superintendent, seeing what was happening and insert-
ing himself in his district's three goals created tension. The superintendent
felt as if he had vowed to work to eliminate disparities whenever he had
influence over decisions. He wanted to improve attendance, discipline, and
achievement outcomes. He was so focused on attaining districtwide clarity
on the goals that he relied less on the team and the power of collaboration
and instead inserted himself into as many conversations as possible. He had
stepped past the role of leader and assumed the role of sole practitioner.

When asked about this, he understood his misstep but defended it initially.
As a superintendent who had been promoted from within his system, he felt
he had a history with so many leaders and teachers in the school district that
he could rely on an open-door approach. What he came to realize was that he
was giving permission to everyone in the system to bypass their supervisors.

He recalled a time when he was asking more and more questions of the
district's chief financial officer (CFO) about the district's marketing program.
The previous superintendent saw an opportunity to fund improvements to
athletics and activities by creating a marketing arm of the school district. It
really interested the superintendent, and he overlooked how it was making the
chief financial officer feel.

Looking back, he realized that it must have been suffocating to have him
asking so many questions in a way that likely sent a message of distrust. An
effective leader considers perspectives, and he hadn't done that. One day, the
CFO came into his office with the big binder she was using to organize the
marketing project and dropped it on his table. "It's yours now," she said.

In the "collective aspiration" section of the human-centered school transformation model, a key component of leadership is having a shared image of
what success looks like. The superintendent and his team hadn't established
a shared image of what a smart and healthy team looked like. Additionally,
shared leadership is a tenet of the "nested pattern" section of the model.
Shared leadership is giving others the authority and autonomy to work on the
goals. The superintendent wasn't sharing leadership. Instead, his actions were
interpreted as being distrustful.

WHAT WAS LEARNED ABOUT RELATIONSHIPS?

As the end of this year approached, the superintendent wrote a journal entry
following a lunch meeting he had attended with the president of a local college. During that meeting, the president talked about leadership and shared

leadership specifically. The superintendent's mind drifted to one of the school district's high schools.

He had been impressed with the active role the teachers and staff played in making their school great. The principal of the high school believed strongly in shared leadership. The principal believed kids were entitled to higher-level courses and worked to find ways to support them. These strongly held beliefs translated into a schoolwide effort to fight for better instructional practices, and the school was recognized statewide and nationally for all it had accomplished.

So when asked about what he learned about relationships, it wasn't about whether or not he was taking time to get to know people. He considered himself a relational leader for most of his career. He saw himself skilled at knowing about people, their families, and their connections to each other. What he learned about relationships is that leaders must not forget the human side of leadership, and they must work to implement predictable processes and practices.

Routines reduce anxiety and confusion. They increase trust in the leader because repeated systems build confidence. From this point on, the superintendent began more regularly using "look, listen, learn, lead," a protocol shared with him by Mark Hansen, a Milwaukee-area superintendent.

Look
State the issue or problem that needs to be resolved.
Listen
Describe the issue or problem fully and without interruption.
Learn
Answer all questions, including system thinking questions like: What would opponents and proponents say? What will this decision look like in one year, three years, five years, and beyond? How long will it take to get the desired results?
Lead
Make a decision and decide how to communicate it.

WHAT WAS FRUSTRATING?

Leaders—especially leaders in public education—routinely hear, "This child will be a third grader only once." That is true. Those who think that school leaders don't think about that all the time are mistaken. School leaders know that illiteracy increases exponentially when a child is not reading on grade level by the end of third grade. They know that the percentage of high school dropouts vastly outnumbers high school graduates in prison (three quarters are illiterate[5] and four fifths have dropped out[6]).

They know the role of a leader is to sometimes disrupt the system. They know how critical it is to make big changes, and at the same time, they want to be in their positions long enough to impact many third-grade cohorts in the years to come.

At this point in this superintendent's career, it was about negotiating and building a coalition. It is what Bolman and Deal[7] refer to as the "political frame." That frustrated this superintendent. So much time must be spent to convince the organization (board of education, central office leaders, principals, and teachers) that the change will make a positive difference in the lives of children (and align with their moral focus). The superintendent found the community's response frustrating as well.

Externally, parents and community members weren't necessarily motivated by the rallying cry of getting kids to school, keeping them in class, and catching them up, because, for the most part, the children in their homes were doing well. They were attending school regularly, staying in school, and performing well on all assessments. Resource allocation to these areas might mean fewer resources for their children. Managing those competing pressures was frustrating for the superintendent.

He started ending his presentations with an image of two people in a boat. On one side of the boat was a hole where the boat was taking on water. On the other side of the boat, noticeably more afloat, the other person says, "Sure glad the hole isn't on my side."

WHAT COULD HAVE BEEN DONE DIFFERENTLY?

In Mary Herrmann's book *Learn to Lead, Lead to Learn*,[8] she advocates for an important tenet of the "leaders' learning work" section of the human-centered school transformational leadership model: serving as the lead learner. What she considers to be an essential leadership trait is to be vulnerable, to admit mistakes, and to be an authentically adaptable leader. In other words, she is describing the characteristics of an imperfect leader.

When asked what could have been done differently, the superintendent wished he had met both individually and as a team with cabinet members to get a better sense of what was working and what wasn't. He wished he had assembled a brain trust of district leaders to better understand what was working and what wasn't. They met regularly, but they weren't positively connected to each other. They lacked clarity.

Clarity is achieved when everyone in an organization uses common language and pursues common goals. The superintendent was moving quickly. Too quickly. He said, "You know that phrase, 'I'm right behind you'? I think they possibly were. Just *really* far behind me."

WHAT WAS SOMETHING GOOD THAT CAME OUT OF THIS EXPERIENCE?

In every industry, leaders are approached by salespeople who promise them the world. I can remember my father telling me about a time when a salesman pitched a new phone system for his office. It wasn't the system that interested my father, but the proposal. "If I save you money," he said, "you pay me half of what I saved you as a one-time fee. But, if you become my client, I will waive the fee. You will save money and I get a new client." My father, an insurance agent, used this method to win over new clients who previously had taken my father's hard work and handed it over to their agents. They saved money and my father got nothing. So whenever a leader can improve the way they approach processes, they should. As part of this experience, the superintendent and the board worked to improve protocols.

First, the board of education elected to conduct a self-assessment. The assessment showed that members felt a small number of board members dominated meetings, that as a whole they didn't demonstrate transparency in their actions, decision making, and communication, and that they didn't believe their colleagues on the board could be trusted with confidential information. This level of distrust bled into the relationship the superintendent had with his bosses as well.

When members of the board of education or members of the administration had ideas about how to improve student experiences or achievement, there was concern that idea would be disregarded. So what would happen is that the idea would be floated at a public meeting. Almost immediately, the media would write an article or include it on the nightly news.

Like wildfire, employees began informally communicating with each other over email, text, and social media and then formally protesting to the board of education or the administration directly. This caused everyone to keep things to themselves, or worse, to work in secret. That only further fomented distrust. The solution came from a local expert in communication and mediation.

She introduced to the superintendent a strategy she called "caterpillar, chrysalis, and butterfly." If they were simply thinking of a new approach or program and wanted to explore that thinking with others, they would simply preface the conversation by saying it was an idea in the "caterpillar stage."

Essentially, they would proceed from leaf to leaf (person to person), learning and thinking.

If, in fact, the idea gained traction, they reframed the idea as being in the "chrysalis stage." It meant that they were bringing more people in, creating a shared image, establishing benchmarks, and discussing budget implications.

If the idea had been considered and all questions answered, then the idea would evolve into the "butterfly stage." It was ready to launch. This simple process proved to be a very successful way of reducing tensions among all groups and especially between board members and the superintendent.

Additionally, the superintendent and his cabinet published a guide, *Building a Collaborative Relationship with the Board of Education*, for the entire organization to follow. They felt this was the best way to put forward innovative ideas or programs. It converted the caterpillar, chrysalis, and butterfly process into a proposed timeline, and it offered a series of prompts for those wishing to advance an innovation for consideration. The superintendent chose to use this model for improving the longstanding process for curriculum adoption.

Even before he became the district's leader, the process for approving curriculum had not changed for a number of years. The school district would put out a request for proposals, and publishers would send the school district a full set of materials to review. A committee of teachers and community members would form, and the materials would be ranked using a rubric. The public would be invited to attend an open house at the district office and provide feedback. The publishers would be available to answer questions.

One year, some board members were not satisfied with the choice, thought it had problems, and publicly questioned the coordinator in charge of the process at a board meeting. The entire district watched in horror. The superintendent was committed to a better process moving forward. Soon after this event, new math materials were being considered by the school district.

Remembering how poorly the previous process had gone, the superintendent spoke about a new process with board members and district leaders. After considering the opportunities and challenges of trying something different, they collectively agreed that it was appropriate to take a more inclusive approach that harvested the wisdom of the people inside and outside the school district.

They would use their scorecard to see which of the comparison districts were doing well in mathematics. They would reach out to the publishers from the top two school districts and invite them to join the project. They would select one school to become the "project school" (the superintendent refused to call it a "pilot" because that term suggests experimentation on people's children).

Every other elementary school would select a project teacher in the primary grades (K–2) and another in the intermediate grades (3–5). The publishers would train teachers and observe lessons. Teachers would meet after each unit and discuss their experiences. They'd use a common assessment after each unit to have a shared image of what success looked like, paying particular attention to students who historically underperformed.

They held regular parent nights to answer questions and gather feedback. Each board member was assigned to a school and would join the superintendent and the coordinators to visit classrooms, observe lessons, and talk to the teachers and principals. The superintendent did this so that every board member could speak personally about what they saw and heard. It made their vote to accept a recommendation well informed. The recommendation would be made by teachers, experts who had used the materials all year long.

Constant feedback loops helped ensure that the collective wisdom was harvested and that leadership was shared. They used this same process when adopting new English language arts materials. When systems include stakeholders—those who are most impacted by decisions—the results are more predictably successful.

When asked for his observations about this experience, it was easy for the superintendent to reflect on the good that came out of this experience. It was the collaboration in decision making, the practice of shared leadership, and a process for communicating possible innovations. This example of collaboration continued to permeate other areas of the organization as well.

What this process helped the superintendent do was to think carefully about proposed innovations. The district wanted to be an organization that had the courage to be creative (innovate), but it also wanted to avoid making impulsive decisions that were costly and time consuming. Impulsiveness breeds distrust.

WATERS CENTER FOR SYSTEMS THINKING HABITS

A Leader Changes Perspectives to Increase Understanding
A Leader Considers an Issue Fully and Resists the Urge to Come to a Quick Conclusion

As you think about your role as a leader, what are some ways you make sure that you are open to other points of view? Who do you approach to help you gain new perspectives on an issue?

One thing that leaders must recognize is that time to consider an issue will lead to better solutions. As we develop as leaders, we have to manage expectations that issues can be resolved immediately. How do you help others be patient while living with an unresolved issue?

NOTES

1. Daniel Boulud, *Letters to a Young Chef* (New York Basic Books, 2017). 121.

2. Patrick M. Lencioni, *The Advantage* (Hoboken, NJ: John Wiley, 2012), 35.

3. Rene S. Townsend, Gloria L. Johnston, Gwen E. Gross, Peggy Lynch, Lorraine Garcy, Benita Roberts, and Patricia B. Novotney, *Effective Superintendent-School Board Practices* (Thousand Oaks, CA: Corwin Press, 2006).

4. Gary L. Anderson, Kathryn Herr, and Ann Sigrid Nihlen, *Studying Your Own School: An Educator's Guide to Qualitative Practitioner Research* (Thousand Oaks, CA: Corwin, 1994), 97.

5. E. Herrick, "Prison Literacy Connection," *Corrections Compendium* 16, no. 12 (1991): 1, 5–9.

6. Matthew Lynch, "High School Dropout Rate: Causes and Costs," *HuffPost*, May 30, 2014, www.huffpost.com/entry/high-school-dropout-rate_b_5421778 (accessed October 22, 2022).

7. Lee G. Bolman and Terrence E. Deal, *Reframing Organizations: Artistry, Choice, and Leadership* (Hoboken, NJ: Jossey-Bass, 1997), 175.

8. Mary B. Herrmann, *Learn to Lead, Lead to Learn* (Lanham, MD: Rowman & Littlefield, 2019).

Chapter 6

Reseeding Their Values

One of my strong points is I make mistakes faster than other people.

—Jim Waters, cofounder of the Waters Center for Systems Thinking

What happened?
A single person choosing the organization's values yields one devout follower.
What got overlooked?
A shared leadership approach will increase your yield.
What was learned about relationships?
People are more connected to each other when they've defined a set of values together.
What was frustrating?
The superintendency is often isolating. Superintendents need to find ways to learn lessons with their teams and not by themselves.
What could have been done differently?
Designing a collaborative process will bring people together.
What was something good that came out of this experience?
The creation of a system for harvesting the wisdom of the organization.

After a superintendent has been in the job for a few years, they think they understand the rhythms and patterns of the job. There are some predictable routines and processes, for sure. There is a sense of confidence in understanding how people behave. These behaviors—the way people in an organization interact with each other—are known as nested patterns. In an organization, this is the muscle of the work. This chapter is about the superintendent embarking on his fourth year and recognizing quickly that it was going to be anything but easy.

His entire cabinet—made up of some of the most veteran leaders in the school district—had left, and he had hired a brand-new cabinet, some of which were hired only a few weeks before the start of the academic year, a difficult time to recruit for school districts. The board of education had just concluded exit interviews with departing cabinet members, and there were threats of lawsuits by leaders who had not been promoted the previous spring. On top of all that, the delay between implemented changes and their expected results was creating tension. The district's data showed discrepancies in both academics and suspensions despite efforts to disrupt the system.

One of the Habits of System Thinking tools created by the Waters Center says, "a systems thinker considers how mental models affect current reality and the future."[1] It felt like everything around this superintendent was falling apart. When he asked a respected leader why the district had a set of values but were not living them, she turned to him and said, "Those values were *your* values, they're not *our* values." She was right. This was a stunning moment for the superintendent. This essential piece—the establishment of the district's values—had been overlooked.

WHAT GOT OVERLOOKED?

When the superintendent was hired, he held an administrator meeting. He planned and planned. He sought advice and counsel from a local business leader, a Baldridge Award[2] recipient, to discuss mission, vision, purpose, and values. He met with his cabinet and revealed nine values that would replace the previous twenty:[3]

- honesty
- transparency
- focus on what works
- mutual respect
- persistence
- teamwork
- positive approach
- adaptability
- commitment

When I say that he met with his cabinet, that is somewhat generous to the superintendent. They haggled as a cabinet a bit over whether the value should be "adaptability" or "flexibility," but other than that, they had very little discussion about them. The superintendent had the values printed on posters and then revealed them, almost like one would imagine Moses at Mount Sinai. So, of course, when things were spinning out of control, in the moment he felt rudderless, the rudder was *his* rudder and not *their* rudder. What was overlooked was the importance of a collaborative process. When leaders include as many voices as possible, they can reasonably expect the organization's culture to be stronger.

WHAT WAS LEARNED ABOUT RELATIONSHIPS?

Have you ever read Jean Giono's *The Man Who Planted Trees*?[4] It's a fictional story with a profound message of persistence and perseverance, of vision and hope. With all of the incredibly difficult distractions this superintendent was experiencing, he wanted to make a midcourse correction and refocus their work. The best way he could think to do that was to tell the following story at the opening meeting of the year.

A man is at a Paris train station at the end of World War I. He is so disturbed by what he has seen that he takes a train to the last stop in the south of France. When he gets off the train, he sees nothing but a desolate landscape. He decides to explore the terrain but soon finds he is running out of water. Desperate for hydration, he approaches a small cabin. In the home lives a solitary man who immediately provides him with food and water. As they talk, the weary traveler asks why the man is living alone in this barren landscape. The hermit smiles and invites him to come with him the following morning.

The next morning, they get up early and head out into the barrenness. They arrive at a spot where the hermit begins planting acorns in the ground. He digs a little hole, places an acorn in the hole, covers it with soil, and waters the spot. The weary traveler, thinking this is beyond foolish, respectfully wishes the hermit well and returns to Paris.

Thirty years later, at the end of World War II, even more distraught by the atrocities he has observed, he takes a train to the final station in the south of France. To his astonishment, he is greeted with a dense forest of oak trees. Immediately, he knows how they got there, and he heads into the forest to look for the man who planted those trees. They are reunited and his belief that one person can make a positive difference is restored.

The superintendent used this story to acknowledge that there are situations—whether it be planting trees or caring for an individual—in which one individual can make a difference. However, when it comes to establishing a healthy organizational culture, this has to be done cooperatively. The values the superintendent originally brought to the district were not the district's values. They should have been a product of the district's collective wisdom, its collective values chosen collaboratively.

The superintendent used the metaphor of a seed as a promise that they would plant a renewed culture that reflected what they wanted for children. They would plant a new culture, one that attended to what they wanted for each other. To do that, they would need to work together, learn to trust each other, and build genuine relationships with each other.

WHAT WAS FRUSTRATING?

The superintendent was most frustrated by falling short. He was frustrated by his failure to consider the basic tenets of appreciative inquiry. Appreciative inquiry is a simple idea and fundamental when considering the kind of school community one might want to create. It challenges leaders to note what is going well and ask how to do more of it. For example, instead of lamenting about why teachers are leaving the district, a leader would look at why they are staying. In this case, the superintendent was asking himself why the organization wasn't following the values instead of asking the better question: what makes people want to follow them?

WHAT COULD HAVE BEEN DONE DIFFERENTLY?

Stavros, Godwin, and Cooperrider state, "At its heart, Appreciative Inquiry (AI) is about the search for the best in people, their organizations, and the strengths-filled, opportunity-rich world around them."[5] The superintendent had failed to do that. He saw his role as that of a leader who would tell people how they should behave. He didn't look back on the twenty values from before he became the superintendent. He didn't approach the work from a strength-based approach. He looked at it as something that needed "fixing." Rather than asking what was wrong, he should have started by asking the team and organization what they valued.

Around this time, teachers and leaders were trying to make sense of the Las Vegas shooting at the Luxor Hotel that left sixty people dead and more than five hundred injured. They watched Hurricane Maria devastate and cripple Puerto Rico, and they mourned the death of a local coach and teacher. In a personal reflection, the superintendent wrote:

> It was like divine intervention. I was tasked with moving some books from a bookshelf and came across one of my texts from graduate school. It wasn't a particularly important book but scrawled on a Post-It note was this quote:

"When you feel like quitting, think about why you started in the first place." I must have written that after a particularly hard day many years earlier when I was a teacher. There were a lot of hard days back then. Extreme poverty, guns, drugs, death, and depression were the norm. But there was also innovation, inspiration, friendship, hope, and love. These past two weeks have been particularly hard locally and for our nation. We've seen some real darkness, which could lead to despair. And at the same time, I've personally witnessed some amazing resiliency from both children and adults. I've seen kindness and compassion. These past two weeks have not been easy by any means. We've had to dig deeper and rely on each other more than ever before.

The superintendent wanted to be a leader who would make progress on issues of poverty. This aligned to his moral focus. Here he was, tripping up on what might be the simple stuff, yet organizational culture is not simple at all. He was working to create a centralized rallying cry in a decentralized system. He made the error, though, of forgetting the importance of a collaborative culture on something as important as their values. It didn't take a lot of introspection to reveal what could have been done differently. He could have engaged in a process that honored the voices and experiences of the organization. That's exactly what the district did. The principal used this moment to engage in an appreciative approach by initiating a collaborative midcourse correction.

WHAT WAS SOMETHING GOOD THAT CAME OUT OF THIS EXPERIENCE?

Recently, I've been interviewing superintendents all over the country about their own experiences. When prompted to provide advice to aspiring or new school leaders, established superintendents often mention mentorship and site visits. Dr. Chris Gaines, a former president of the American Association of School Administrators,[6] told me that finding a mentor and rubbing elbows with other leaders are some of the most important improvement strategies. This is exactly what the superintendent did.

He took a team to visit a comparative school district to consider how to go about creating a more collaborative structure. The agenda for the visit included a presentation by the host superintendent, a brief tour of a program or project they were proud of, and then a few hours with their counterparts. The superintendents would spend time together while the chief financial officers and assistant superintendents would do the same. This gave them all the opportunity to have real conversations with leaders walking in similar shoes.

While the superintendents were together, the superintendent asked his host for advice on how to build and maintain consistency of message. His host told him about his regular meetings with all his district's leaders. They would first conduct a leadership training, and then they would work together to tackle an issue facing the school district. Loving this idea, the superintendent began planning a meeting to reseed their values.

The superintendent created a leadership council and invited teachers (selected by their professional associations), students, principals, assistant principals, directors, supervisors, curriculum coordinators, social workers, and professionals from nutrition services, custodial, and facilities and construction to help him be a lead learner. He wanted an opportunity to acknowledge his mistake and to ask the organization to learn alongside him.

A PROCESS FOR HARVESTING THE WISDOM OF THE ORGANIZATION

Harvesting the collective wisdom of an organization is essential to shared leadership. Knowing what people think and why they think a certain way produces feelings of inclusion and acceptance. With the help of a mentor, the superintendent crafted a process that included the many voices represented in the large organization. The first thing he did was to ask people to think about a value that was important to them and to write it down on a piece of paper.

Then, he asked everyone to stand up and find another person from another table. They would each have two minutes to talk about the value they chose. Next, he asked them to take a moment to write a quick reflection about what they had just heard from their peers.

He asked them to find another person in the room and share their value, as well as the value shared by their previous partner. This was followed by one more opportunity to write and reflect on these two conversations. Those conversations were focused and productive. A number of participants confessed to changing their initial value based on those interactions.

Next, the superintendent asked everyone to return to their tables and to take ten minutes to share their values with each other. At this point, he asked each table to choose one value to represent it (they were encouraged to have a backup as well just in case another table chose the same value). There were nearly thirty tables, which meant they collected thirty unduplicated values. They wrote them on poster paper, placed them around the room, and read the list of values aloud.

Participants were asked to advocate for a value on the list. It was important to make it clear that this was not a debate, but an opportunity to explain why they were so connected to a particular value. After about twenty minutes of individuals spontaneously sharing their reasons for including a value, the group moved to the final step of the process.

Each participant received three sticker dots, which represented three votes. Each person was asked to vote for the most important value or values (using their dots in any way they chose). The dots were tallied during a break and the list was revealed to the entire group. Their new values would be:

- trust
- integrity
- collaboration
- transparency
- empathy
- grace

As the superintendent looked around the room, he realized something profound about the collaborative process they had just concluded. Together, they had made a commitment. Together, they made a promise to each other that these agreed-upon values would serve them when things were going well and buoy them when things were tough.

A few months later, they delved deeper into their new values. Once again harvesting the wisdom of the room, they worked together collaboratively to generate a shared image for each value. It's one thing to vote on six values, but it's another thing to define them. Here they are again, with their definitions:

Trust—believe firmly in the ability of others to do their part to achieve our shared vision and values.

Integrity—demonstrate the courage to always act for what is good and right for all stakeholders.

Collaboration—welcome the contribution of each individual and understand that together we make meaningful and lasting decisions.

Transparency—practice intentional clarity with all communication to create a culture where all people feel valued for their opinions and feel safe to ask questions.

Empathy—seek to understand others and their unique viewpoints.

Grace—presume that all persons operate with positive intent and forgive mistakes.

When asked to talk about what this experience meant to him, the superintendent described it as a major transitional moment. Until that point, he had felt more like a steward of the superintendents who came before him. He recognized the importance of standing on the shoulders of those who came before him. All leaders must do that. Everything until this point, though, was a continuation of previous administrations. That continuity of mission was important. There's no doubt that a leader must honor previous plans.

However, without attending to the very foundation—the organization's nested patterns and values—a leader risks being perpetually off balance.

In this chapter, we find a leader stepping out of the shadows of his predecessor in a meaningful way. Through high levels of collaboration and positive connectedness, he has designed better systems to harvest the collective wisdom of the organization. In this chapter, we are reintroduced to the superintendent as a leader more willing to shed his uncertainties and more bravely living the principles of the model for human-centered school transformation.

WATERS CENTER FOR SYSTEMS THINKING HABITS

A Leader Considers How Mental Models Affect Current Reality and the Future
A Leader Identifies the Circular Nature of Complex Cause-and-Effect Relationships

The superintendent's challenge in this chapter required him to step back and recognize how his actions deprived the organization of creating shared nested patterns together. As a leader, how could your own mental models be barriers to what you are trying to achieve?

Causal loops are ways to understand how parts of a system are connected. For the superintendent, when collaboration increased, trust also increased. As trust increased, opportunities to collaborate increased. How do parts affect one another in your organization?

NOTES

1. "Waters Center for Systems Thinking," Waters Center for Systems Thinking, https://thinkingtoolsstudio.waterscenterst.org/cards (accessed October 21, 2022).

2. Paul Hernandez, "Baldrige Performance Excellence Program," NIST, last modified April 11, 2019, www.nist.gov/baldrige.

3. Previous values included: student achievement as the priority; elimination of achievement disparities; equitable curriculum and learning opportunities to prepare all students for citizenship, careers, and college; learner engagement; diversity; highly qualified staff; professionalism; collaboration; innovation; data-driven decisions; a culture of dignity; a safe learning environment; quality facilities; appropriate instructional resources; adequate technology resources and support; partnerships between schools, parents, and the entire Columbia community; open, proactive communication; visionary leadership; excellent fiscal management and accountability; and efficient, judicious use of public resources.

4. Jean Giono, *The Man Who Planted Trees* (New York: Random House, 2015).

5. Jacqueline M. Stavros, Lindsey N. Godwin, and David L. Cooperrider, "Appreciative Inquiry," in *Practicing Organization Development*, ed. William J. Rothwell, Jackie Stavros, and Roland L. Sullivan, 96–116 (Hoboken, NJ: John Wiley, 2015).

6. AASA, the School Superintendents Association, www.aasa.org/home/ (accessed October 22, 2022).

Chapter 7

A Tree Takes Root

He who plants a tree, plants hope.

—Lucy Carcom

What happened?
A middle school gay-straight alliance club created posters and parents protested.

What got overlooked?
Without clear communication, there is confusion, frustration, and anxiety.

What was learned about relationships?
A facilitated conversation can help build understanding.

What was frustrating?
Past progress doesn't automatically translate into credibility.

What could have been done differently?
Those impacted by a decision should be active participants in the decision.

What was something good that came out of this experience?
After-action reviews are a valuable practice for an organization as they build trust.

Each year, at the beginning of the school year, Jewish families attend synagogue to observe Rosh Hashanah, the Jewish New Year. On Rosh Hashanah—or the head of the year in Hebrew—they reflect on the past year. They consider the decisions they've made and the actions they've taken. They think about their friendships and their families, and they think about the year ahead.

There is an important component to the day, too: the sounding of the sho-far. A shofar is a ram's horn, which is blown like a trumpet. Used in biblical times to rally armies, it has a modern function. The shofar's blast is an awak-ening. It calls a congregation to action.

The superintendent experiences his own awakening in this chapter. As he looked back over the years of the superintendency, he marveled at how much the district had accomplished. In a letter to district leaders, he told them that he was looking forward to the work they had ahead of them. He told them he was imagining their collective call to action. Essentially, he was thinking about the model for human-centered school transformational leadership with its collective aspiration, nested patterns, and leaders' learning work.

He told them he felt called to keep working on behalf of the children in the district, especially when it came to their goals of getting children to school, keeping them in class, catching them up, and extending them further. He remained committed to the equity work with the district's leaders leading that work.

In the previous chapter, the process of convening a leadership council meeting with the school district's leaders led to a major transition from the superintendent's values to the district's values. Leadership council meetings became an important part of the superintendent's leadership model. The meet-ings lasted one hour and included a short presentation by the superintendent followed by an opportunity to engage in high-level collaboration on a variety of topics.

He started the meetings with the human-centered school transformation model, paying close attention to collective aspiration and its embedded tenet, shared images of success. He shared pictures from school visits. Seeing teachers working closely with children and celebrating staff collaboration highlighted the good things happening in the school district. Then he ask the council members to read or watch something related to leadership, and they processed the themes individually and collectively. Finally, he asked for their help on issues facing the school district. One example was snow days.

If you're a school leader and you live in a state with winter weather, you know how difficult it is to call a snow day. Until the global pandemic, it was the worst decision superintendents had to make because they are lose-lose propositions. Half of your community will agree with your decision while the other half will disagree, often loudly. The superintendent was looking for ways to put a more collaborative culture into practice. Snow days and the pro-cess for considering a school closure seemed like a good topic. In asking for advice on how best to communicate snow days, the leadership council asked the superintendent to first describe the process used by the school district. Principals, for example, are the first ones contacted by parents and staff, and they couldn't always explain how the decision was made.

The superintendent asked them if they remembered the previous winter's week of school closures due to snow. Everyone nodded. He remarked that at the end of that difficult week, on that Sunday morning, while he and his son trudged through the predawn snow, his neighbors peered from their windows. He laughed a little as he noted, "We *never* see our neighbors during the winter, but this weekend, they were waiting for us!"

"Mr. Superintendent," one called out, "there better be school on Monday!" Another neighbor declared, "If you don't take them tomorrow, you're home schooling my kids at *your* house!" Leadership council members chuckled. The superintendent continued.

He said, "During the five snow days, most children were unaware of the consternation experienced by parents throughout the community. I'm sure many loved having extended screen time. Truthfully, I couldn't stop thinking of an adaptation of that old 'This is your brain' public service announcement. But in this case, it was 'This is your brain on Minecraft.'"

The superintendent recalled moments with his own children that week that were incredibly charming. The boys wanted to create individualized Valentine charms for their classmates and so they set out to design bracelets with personalized messages. All was going well until the youngest child began arguing with the middle child about the excessive use of the letter *E*. As they bickered, the oldest child quietly strung together a four-letter word and slid his creation across the table to his mother: *H-E-L-P*. Cabin fever was making everyone weary. Even the superintendent's sons wanted to know when they could get back to school.

A school principal raised her hand and said she was stopped in the produce area of the local grocery store by a parent who genuinely wanted to understand how the decision was made. She related what the parent said: "I really do believe that the school district is making the best decision for students, but from our perspective, it seems like we're not going to school when it seems like we could." The principal added, "She wanted to know what we consider when deciding school closings. I think that's a fair question."

The superintendent paused. The question was a fair question. It also revealed the new culture taking root. Shared leadership means explaining your thinking. It means embracing a growth mindset and being willing to adjust your thinking. In this case, he needed to reconsider the hierarchy of leadership he had known previously.

He described being part of the 4:30 a.m. team that drove the roads to determine whether or not to have school. His route encompassed mostly the community's downtown area. Each time the team reconvened at 5:30, each member shared his or her experiences. The superintendent recalled that he almost always blurted out, "Let's have school." But then he'd hear what the other team members had endured. Driving the rural roads, which were mostly gravel and the first to freeze, was almost always dreadful. The roads on the outskirts of the suburban areas often were described as treacherous and the neighborhoods sitting on bluffs were simply impassable.

What the superintendent learned from being on that driving team was the massive size of the district. As a moderately large district, it transported almost nine thousand students in more than two hundred buses every day. The miles those buses traveled created a significant hurdle when it snowed. Additionally, when the temperatures were consistently below zero, the bus fuel lines, especially in older buses, ran the risk of freezing. So the superintendent described how he looked at the urban, suburban, and rural parts of the school district. He explained how he looked at existing precipitation and outdoor temperatures. He considered when sunrise would be and what that meant for kids waiting at bus stops and inexperienced teenagers driving to school. He said, "The thought of a five-year-old waiting outside for a bus that might never come is a compelling reason to delay or cancel school."

The superintendent paused and reiterated his request to the leadership council for its counsel. A high school principal raised her hand and said, "I think I can speak for my colleagues here today. It appears so much goes into the decision, but until today, I didn't have a clue. My suggestion would be to put your thinking into an email and send it out to parents at the same time the decision is made. That way, we can forward it to parents who ask us." Her colleagues nodded. They suggested that the superintendent also post the thinking behind the decision on social media, too.

The conversation was such a powerful experience that the superintendent brought a new topic to a subsequent leadership council. This time it was not an operations question, but a collective aspiration one. He wanted the council's help in defining what access to academic achievement meant for children in their school district.

First, the leaders worked individually on the question before finding someone else in the room to talk to. After processing with that partner, they met up with another leader in the room to share their thinking. Then all leaders returned to their tables to talk with their colleagues. Each table was tasked with writing a sentence on poster paper and hanging it on the wall.

The superintendent invited everyone to take a gallery walk, a process of quietly reading what others have written. At each poster, a representative remained to explain their table's thinking. There were markers by each poster for additional questions or suggested edits. Before concluding the session, a leader read their table's definition for what achievement meant, along with any additions, deletions, and edits.

At the next leadership council, the superintendent gave the council members sticker dots and asked them to vote for their top six definitions. They collectively chose the following definitions:

- Achievement means we intervene early enough to change the outcome.
- Achievement means systems are in place to guarantee children are getting what they need (academically and behaviorally).
- Achievement means all children have access to a high-quality interdisciplinary curriculum, including a place-based and culturally responsive education.
- Achievement means we strive to ensure all children are socially, emotionally, and physically healthy.
- Achievement means high-quality, job-embedded professional development for all teachers led by local talent (our own people).
- Achievement means we provide fair, accurate, specific, and timely information regarding student progress toward agreed-upon common standards.

These definitions, written and confirmed by the district's leaders, would become the anchors for instructional, staffing, and budgetary decisions. The superintendent described the work as incredibly rewarding. A working assumption of the human-centered school transformation model is that "one of a leader's most important roles is to nurture a rich cultural field that supports learning for every person in the school system."[1] Whether it was making an operational decision or an instructional one, that's exactly what the superintendent was doing. A culture of deeper learning was taking root.

A STRONG WIND TESTS THE ROOTS

The superintendent used the power of language and built upon the seed metaphor. He used a tree to show that their seeds had taken root and were beginning to grow. In an email to all district employees, he shared these words:

> As symbols of growth and strength, trees start out with shallow roots that strengthen and grow deeper over time. But not without care and support. Just like a tree, a person grows stronger over time and strives for greater knowledge and new experiences. Trees are deeply connected to the world and dependent on that world to grow and thrive. The same for people. The same for your colleagues. The same for our students.

A month after the superintendent sent that message out, the sponsor of a middle school gay-straight alliance (GSA) hung student-made posters in hallways throughout the building. The posters, resembling the "Got Milk?" campaign, presented celebrities and definitions of terms associated with their LGBTQ+

identities. The poster project became a disruption for the community, a split down ideological lines.

It was the beginning of October, and it had taken about two weeks before the posters were brought to the superintendent's attention. At the end of the second week, he was getting calls and emails to remove the posters. The protests kept referring to them as "curriculum."

The superintendent didn't oppose the posters, nor did he consider them instructional materials. He was, however, somewhat persuaded by some parents who said their children didn't understand what the posters meant. Since parents weren't told about them going up, they could only try to understand what they were. They were relying on their middle school children.

Some parents were appropriate in their correspondence and offered suggestions to honor the work of the children who created the posters. Many parents were not so considerate or thoughtful. One notable call came from a well-connected community member:

PARENT: Doctor, my son is not a good athlete, he doesn't know where he fits in, and when he sees these posters, he's going to think, "Hey, maybe I'm gay."

SUPERINTENDENT: Am I talking to you as the superintendent or as someone who has known you for a long time?

PARENT: You know me. I'm old school; you can say anything you want.

SUPERINTENDENT: That's not how it works!

Needless to say, the parent and the superintendent didn't see eye to eye on the posters. What happened next, though, created some confusion and frustration as the superintendent worked to find middle ground.

WHAT GOT OVERLOOKED?

The posters were created by the students of the gay-straight alliance, an organization with close ties to other school clubs like the Fellowship of Christian Athletes. They were created as part of LGBT History Month (a lot of correspondence received was about Pride Month, which is in June). The posters were to complement a timeline of historic LGBT events already posted near the school's main entrance.

Initially, during a phone call with the teacher sponsor, the superintendent told her that she could keep the posters up. Then two parents asked to meet with the superintendent on a Friday, to which he agreed. The principal of the middle school notified the superintendent that she was leaving town for the weekend, so he said the district's chief equity officer would represent her at the meeting.

In an effort to hold a restorative meeting,[2] they agreed to some norms and that they'd all work to find common ground and a reasonable solution. Initially, the parents demanded the removal of the posters that day. The superintendent reminded them that it was Friday and said the children who created the posters would feel betrayed and rejected if they left on a Friday only to find the posters gone on Monday.

He proposed taking them down by the end of the following week and moving them to a central location where their purpose and context could be better understood and appreciated. There was already a display on the history of the rainbow LGBT pride flag by the gymnasium, so the posters could go there, keeping them in a prominent spot and not hiding them from view.

What the superintendent didn't fully appreciate was that the principal was getting besieged by parents. She told him that she had decided the posters needed to be removed entirely. The superintendent told her that he supported her decision. With close to forty school buildings in the school district, he believed that principals should have the authority and autonomy to make decisions about things they deem an interruption to the learning environment. This decision created confusion and frustration, internally and externally.

Looking back at what got overlooked, the superintendent should not have had the meeting without the principal and sponsor. They would have had clearer communication had they been in the room together. Additionally, when they reached an oral agreement with the parents about moving the posters, they should have written it down formally and signed it. One of the parents later called the superintendent angry that the posters were not permanently removed but instead relocated.

WHAT WAS LEARNED ABOUT RELATIONSHIPS?

It wasn't until the superintendent took a moment to reflect on this experience that he considered how relationships can be damaged if a leader fails to establish a shared image for communication and problem solving. He shared his journal entry:

> This week, I grew as a leader. It's interesting how, just like with the growth spurts of our kids, leadership development has a comparable excruciating feeling. You're up at night tossing and turning. You're somewhat inconsolable. People can empathize, but they don't know exactly what you're going through.

Whatever I was feeling this week from a system level was nothing compared to one of our principals. I felt like a FEMA director answering questions and directing media from a central location (as well as visiting the site to check on things in person). The principal was like the mayor of a community before, during, and after a storm. She was comforting, reassuring, and trying to inspire others.

I know each principal is dealing with high emotional issues each and every day. This one was complex because a clear delineation between school and district kept being blurred by stakeholders. This one was a doozy. And it taught me a lot about how to be a better superintendent.

A month or so after writing this, the superintendent called the sponsor of the school's gay-straight alliance club and the principal to ask if they would participate in an after-action review (AAR) with him. Since he would be a participant, he proposed they invite a facilitator to help them. They agreed.

On the day of the AAR, each of the participants took turns giving their perspectives. They expressed how they felt about the situation, including how they felt supported (or not). Because the participants agreed that they would not share what others said during the AAR, the actual statements cannot appear in this book, but when asked about the experience, the superintendent said he experienced the district value of giving grace (forgiveness). He sought it from both the sponsor and the principal. The experience helped him appreciate even more fully the power of human-centered leadership.

WHAT WAS FRUSTRATING?

During his first year as the district's leader, the superintendent worked with board members and community advocates to propose and pass additional protections to its antidiscrimination policy. They added gender identity and expression to a policy that already included sexual orientation as a protected class. Since their state was (and continues to be) a state where it is legal to fire someone for being gay, it was an important part of their equity agenda to extend and expand protections to the school district's three thousand employees and nineteen thousand children.

The district took a great deal of heat from some members of their community, including from a locally elected state representative. He came to the podium and remarked that the school district talked about tolerance and acceptance but questioned why his granddaughters have to tolerate or accept this kind of behavior. So when social media posts about the middle school posters pitted neighbor against neighbor and friend against friend, it was incredibly frustrating. It was frustrating for the superintendent who became a target of some of the comments. It was frustrating that the work he had been actively involved in early in his superintendency was not recognized and respected by those disappointed in how he handled the situation.

WHAT COULD HAVE BEEN DONE DIFFERENTLY?

One of the most important things leaders need to pay attention to is the different perspectives and roles within their organization. If leaders say that they believe in shared leadership but fail to include those most impacted by the decision, then really what they are perpetuating is a traditional model of leadership. Leading solely in a hierarchical structure is the antithesis of a human-centered leadership model.

Looking back on this experience, the superintendent was able to perch on the balcony of this scenario and clearly see what could have been done differently. He could have ensured the sponsor and the principal were at his side from the very beginning. Although he thought he was representing their interests well, they weren't in the room. They couldn't know what was being discussed and decided. The superintendent wasn't the sponsor of the gay-straight alliance. He didn't have a right to speak for the sponsor or the student members. The principal, the sponsor, and the students were forced to learn about the compromise and agreement from the superintendent, and they had a difficult time defending the decisions because they weren't a part of the decision process.

WHAT WAS SOMETHING GOOD THAT
CAME OUT OF THIS EXPERIENCE?

One day, a report came in that a bus filled with elementary students was involved in a head-on collision with a single driver. The driver of the vehicle reportedly crossed into oncoming traffic and hit the bus. County fire and emergency management teams were dispatched. The assistant superintendent and superintendent raced to the scene. En route, they learned that another bus had been sent to the scene to transport all the children to the local hospital for assessment. They headed to the hospital.

Parents were notified and the media was informed. A regular set of updates was prepared for the board of education and the public. Every child was safe. Not one required additional medical attention. Tragically, the driver of the vehicle died at the scene.

A week after the event, everyone involved in the response that day assembled in a hospital conference room to review the actions in an AAR process. The superintendent had never been involved in such a well-structured review of an incident. He was so impressed with the way the meeting was facilitated, the great care taken to ensure every detail was discussed. He hoped, one day, it would become a common practice for the school district.

The power of the AAR process following the gay-straight alliance poster situation inspired the superintendent to utilize it more frequently. The process of learning how each person experienced a situation demonstrated a high point in his career. Although the issue wasn't completely resolved to everyone's satisfaction, a genuine appreciation for each individual's perspective (and lived experiences) was respected. Something good that came from this experience and what was learned from this experience was the power of the after-action review protocol.

WATERS CENTER FOR SYSTEMS THINKING HABITS

A Leader Considers Short-Term, Long-Term, and Unintended Consequences of Actions
A Leader Considers an Issue Fully and Resists the Urge to Come to a Quick Conclusion

In this chapter, the superintendent made a few short-term decisions before contemplating the long-term implications.

In your role as a leader, think about a decision you've recently made. What are the possible long- and short-term consequences of the proposed action? How might you respond if they come to pass? How will you help others to be patient while living with unresolved issues?

NOTES

1. "A Model for Human-Centered School Transformation," Santa Fe Center for Transformational School Leadership, https://transformationalschoolleadership .com/transformationleadership/model-for-human-centered-school-transformation/ (accessed October 21, 2022).

2. "What Is Restorative Practices?" International Institute for Restorative Practices, www.iirp.edu/restorative-practices/what-is-restorative-practices (accessed October 22, 2022).

Chapter 8

They Know the Way—Until a Pandemic Emerges

Authenticity is a collection of choices that we have to make every day. It's about the choice to show up and be real. The choice to be honest. The choice to let our true selves be seen.

—Brene Brown

What happened?
The school district shifted from a traditional school year to one interrupted by a global pandemic.
What got overlooked?
A shared image of what feedback looks like.
What was learned about relationships?
When you are looking for negativity, you will find it. When instead you seek out examples of positive connectedness, you will easily find them, too.
What was frustrating?
In a decentralized system, there are plenty of opportunities for confusion and anger.
What could have been done differently?
Don't undervalue how looking for additional listening opportunities could have built goodwill.
What was something good that came out of this experience?
It is a marvelous thing when a community comes together.

There's a Chinese tale about two wandering priests walking through the countryside. During their travels, they come upon a traversable but still somewhat treacherous stream. At the water's edge stands an elderly woman. Without hesitation, the older and wiser of the two priests offers the woman safe passage across by inviting her to climb onto his back. The entire time across the stream, the elderly woman complains and criticizes the experienced priest.

"You're not walking fast enough!"

"I'm getting splashed. Be more careful!"

"This isn't help. This is torture!"

They finally arrive at the other end. The priest gently kneels down and the woman carelessly dismounts. The older priest strains as he rises but still maintains a calm disposition and, in fact, makes an effort to bow to the woman.

Throughout this episode, the other priest, younger and inexperienced, has watched with shock and bewilderment. How did his traveling companion manage to stay so disciplined and focused on service and self-sacrifice during this ordeal?

As the two continued their journey, the younger priest could not shake the day's events from his mind. At every turn, he would say things like:

"Can you believe that woman? What nerve!"

"Was she not grateful for your good deed?"

"I don't know about you, but I probably would have dropped her in the water and kept walking!"

After about an hour or two of these periodic outbursts by the younger priest, his far wiser mentor and friend turned to him and said, "I stopped carrying the old woman nearly two hours ago. My friend, why are *you* still carrying her?"

This story is a parable for the superintendency. So often district leaders find themselves distracted by issues that seem insurmountable at the time but that are inconsequential in the grand scheme of things. There are so many things that superintendents just need to let go.

The story is also about empathy and grace, two of this school district's values. The wise older priest practiced empathy and grace when he considered the woman's plight and circumstances. These would be qualities that the superintendent would look to as the year started typically and ended with a global pandemic.

The story is about two worlds. One world, an old world, where obligations to others are respected and expected. And another world, one built more on self-interest. One that is built on a mentality that my children are mine and not ours. A world where challenges and obstacles are not necessarily tackled as a community. That became even more clear for the superintendent as the year went on.

The superintendent launched the year with a meeting to highlight the values (seeds) they had planted previously. He referenced the saplings (examples of the values being practiced) that had taken root. In fact, he noted that a dense forest had emerged and that they would need a compass to find their way. He gave everyone a gift, a compass as a touchstone of the journey they were on together.

He dimmed the lights and projected the image of a person in a canoe. The water was placid, representing the calm waters where they now found themselves. In the distance was a lighted dock, their destination. When they arrived there, they'd find their two most important areas of focus:

- A fair and equitable system of teaching and learning.
- A system for intervening when children struggled.

It was such a powerful meeting from his perspective because it represented the beginning of a third year of consistent progress. Additionally, in an effort to find new ways to engage parents and community members, he praised the school district's equity department for launching Parent-Community University. They conducted a number of sessions, many of them facilitated by students:

- What does access look like in the district?
- How does the school district measure and determine student progress?
- How does the school district provide a full educational experience (extra-curricular activities, academic enrichment, and intervention supports)?
- How does the school district help students plan and prepare for the future?

Each session was recorded so that it could also be watched on demand. The theme for the year was "We Know the Way," and the superintendent wanted to make sure the path was clear for the community as well.

In fact, he was feeling really good about a lot of things during this year. In January, the school district's chief financial officer led a collaborative session with all district leaders that focused on prioritizing their upcoming budget. They harvested the collective wisdom of the more than 125 participants and determined that instructional supports and mental health supports were highly valued.

As they made decisions for the district's children, they did it with their two priorities in mind: helping schools give children the best chance at academic learning and helping them build systems of support when it came to the mental health concerns of their children.

If that meant more resources at one school than at another, the superintendent was comfortable doing that as long as the decision was made with those two goals in mind and according to the shared values created by the school district. They were showing how transparency, trust, integrity, empathy, collaboration, and grace were not just words. They continued to be a promise. They were all on the same page. They had a shared image of a successful budget.

In early March, the district launched Early College, which enabled high school juniors and seniors to enroll in a local community college to complete both their high school diploma and associate's degree at the same time. High school students retained all rights and privileges to their high schools and were able to attend college at no cost. The school district would be reimbursed for a student's attendance in the program, and it would pay the student's reduced college tuition with those funds.

School district staff had hoped that 50 students would consider Early College and were overjoyed when 126 enrolled in the program. Early College was a game changer for families trying to figure out how to pay for college, and the relationship between the community college and state universities ensured complete course alignment. Students would be able to enter a state college or university with two years of credit and all of their college prerequisites completed.

Then the superintendent started hearing about a virus spreading in Seattle and New York. He wrote a note in his journal that the district should plan to give an update on the emerging coronavirus at the April board meeting. In mid-March, however, he held a meeting with the director of the local health department. It became abundantly clear that his presentation would be earlier than April. It would be an explanation as to why the virus would be closing the district.

In advance of the meeting, he responded to questions from community members. They wanted to know how this year was different from past years when there were high cases of the flu. He was preparing for these questions. In previous years, he thought, people were not directed to stay in their homes by every level of national, state, and local government. In previous years, they were not tuning in to the news or talking with neighbors who had been impacted in some way by a global pandemic. In previous years, they hadn't experienced such tremendous loss. He hoped for a return to normal routines. Everyone else was hoping for that, too. Unfortunately, like school districts all across the globe, each decision caused more and more grief.

The weeks after the April meeting were followed by decisions about proms, graduations, summer school, and summer professional development. The superintendent and school board discussed the possibility of returning to buildings to close out the academic year, something that soon became an impossibility. They turned their attention to the next school year and began making plans for what a robust return might look like. The superintendent knew he would need a human-centered structure to honor the many internal perspectives. He put into action a process he had learned previously, a method to harvest the collective wisdom of the organization.

AN INCIDENT COMMAND STRUCTURE PROCESS

A year earlier, the superintendent was determined to create a third assistant superintendent position. He was convinced what needed to be done was to create three distinct area districts. Each assistant superintendent would become an area superintendent responsible for the three comprehensive high schools and the preschools, elementary schools, and middle schools that fed into them. He proposed the idea to the board of education. He called a meeting with his leaders to share the idea and to ask for feedback. The process they used turned out to be one of the best collaborative tools for harvesting the collective wisdom of the organization.

Prior to the meeting, the superintendent asked respected thought leaders from every level of the organization to participate in a conversation about the plan. As they talked, the rest of the district's leaders sat in a large circle observing the conversation. Some organizational leaders refer to this as a "fishbowl" structure, with an inner circle of participants and an outer circle of observers. He intentionally left one open chair in the inner circle for anyone from the outer circle to temporarily join to ask a question or make a comment.

The superintendent shared his proposal and responded to questions and concerns. Leaders sat in the open chair and asked additional questions. The organization helped him get to the crux of his issue. He didn't really want to break up the school district and disrupt its efforts to become one centralized school district. Instead, it was pointed out, what he really wanted was to create a more responsive cabinet while also finding ways to build better cohesion between the elementary and secondary levels. The feedback led to a better decision. Following the session, he wrote the participants a note:

> A culture of deep learning stresses shared decision making. Four years ago, I likely would have pushed forward on my own. I want to be the kind of leader who is responsive, thoughtful, and purposeful. You helped me consider ways to do that. When we next get together, I want that time together to help us take a step closer to the kind of culture we planted last year and are cultivating this year.

As it became clear that the pandemic would not be a two-week interruption of the school year, this experience, along with the budget planning meeting, were cited as reasons why leaders trusted the superintendent's ability to establish an incident command structure during the pandemic. He had shown an ability to listen, adapt, and use their feedback to make human-centered decisions.

As the head of a large organization with close to forty buildings and thousands of employees responsible for thousands of children, the superintendent had experience practicing an incident command structure. This was part of the cabinet's annual training for possible natural or man-made disasters. With a nuclear reactor in the local community and a full-fledged nuclear power plant a little more than twenty miles away, the district met regularly with local emergency management teams for simulations. The superintendent recognized the emergence of COVID-19 as a reason to authorize an incident command structure. He began convening 125 leaders to a weekly meeting. From the very first meeting, he insisted on reading the district's values:

- Integrity
- Trust
- Transparency
- Collaboration
- Empathy
- Grace

He remembered emphasizing that they'd make mistakes as they went along and that they would lean on the value of grace regularly. He was highlighting how he'd model imperfect leadership as he tried to navigate a global pandemic last experienced in 1918.

Additionally, the superintendent established norms for the weekly meeting. As incident commander, he wanted to make a few expectations clear. Each week, he read the following four norms:

- This is serious.
- Work together.
- Disagree politely.
- Accept and support the final decision.

He also established a protocol for keeping the board of education informed. Following every meeting, he called the board president, vice president, or senior member of the board. He knew communication with the board was essential. In fact, after a few weeks, he began inviting a member of the board of education to listen to the weekly conversation and offer his or her gratitude to the leaders on the call.

At about that same time, he began inviting a small group of principals to participate in the incident command meetings. He met with this brain trust an hour before each incident command meeting so he could seek their counsel in advance. Principals were the ones most responsible for the district's success when it came to consistency of practice and messaging to teachers and staff. To have their advice and feedback in advance proved to be invaluable.

To give an idea of the scope of what they were trying to accomplish, here is a list of questions from one of their first meetings:

1. How will we treat sick days when an employee gets COVID-19?
2. Teachers are being told to stay home. Should staff come in?
3. What happens when a staff member says their spouse is sick and he or she stays home?
4. The Centers for Disease Control (CDC) says that if your school notices a substantial increase in the number of students or staff missing school due to illness, report this to your local health officials. What is considered "substantial"?
5. Will curriculum coordinators work on a menu of options for teachers and parents (including English learners and special education)? Can we survey kids to find out who has internet services?
6. Who will order three hundred additional hot spots?
7. People are being reminded to stay out of emergency rooms if possible. Can we remind people about telemedicine?
8. The CDC says to evaluate whether there are students or staff who are at increased risk of severe illness and to develop plans for them to continue to work or receive educational services if there is moderate levels of COVID-19 transmission or impact. Who will do this?
9. The National Education Association (NEA) wants to survey all staff. Can we conduct an additional survey asking if people need to care for ill parents/children?
10. How will this affect our school calendar? Will we need to make up school days?
11. What is the tipping point for starting a modified instructional programming?
12. What is the percentage of absences that we can absorb for staff? Students?
13. Can we suspend professional development to prioritize staffing levels?
14. Can we even do online classes? Online learning at all levels? Are there resources to consider using?
15. What would online learning look like?
16. Would we close one school or the entire school district?
17. What about food for free/reduced lunch students?
18. Will buses be sanitized after each route?
19. Do we need to increase the areas where we supply hand sanitizer? Computer labs? Locker rooms? Docks? Libraries?
20. Do we have enough soap?
21. If students with disabilities are diagnosed with COVID-19, what will their homebound/hospital services look like?

22. What additional precautions should be taken for students with already compromised immune systems?

23. How will we know if students who have recently arrived from other countries completed the recommended self-quarantine period? Do we need to postpone enrollment for fourteen days after we know about their need to enroll?

24. What happens if this is a long-term situation regarding the administration of state testing?

25. Do we have a centralized communication plan for employees who do not access email regularly?

26. What if staff and students travel during spring break (or on weekends) and come back sick? What do we do?

27. Partners and satellite locations (for example, Boys and Girls Club and Juvenile Justice Center) need advice. What guidance can the district provide to help them make decisions about whether to be open or closed, in person or virtual?

28. Will we have athletic events? If yes, what about fans? Media?

29. Can we add mental health services?

TEACHER AND STAFF PARTICIPATION

The superintendent also wanted to know what teachers and staff thought. Transparency was one of the school district's values, and he wanted to find another way to stay engaged with his colleagues. He wrote a note to them.

Lately, the use of metaphor has been used to help capture different aspects of our current situation:

"It will not be a switch we just turn back on; it'll be a dial."

"If we see an uptick in cases, it will not be just slowing the car down, but more like turning the car around and starting the trip from the very beginning."

"If you think about it, we're not a kayak, but more like an ocean liner (and sometimes it feels as if everyone on the ocean liner has cast their own anchor into the sea!)."

We're all trying to make sense of a situation that makes very little sense. We've been lucky as a community to have relatively few cases, and yet surrounding counties and cities across the state have not been as fortunate. We know the only way we can fight this thing is with social distancing. We know we've been asked to follow the guidelines established by the health department, and we intend to do just that. We know there are many questions about high school graduations as well as many other questions. For those questions, we have created a document to share what we *know*, collect questions from employees about *what* they want to know, and provide answers on what we have *learned* (KWL).

Every single superintendent in the nation was wrestling with these types of questions. Each question brought on a new set of questions. It was an undertaking with very little preparation.

The superintendent started every incident command meeting with updates from the cabinet. Then he asked each department head for an update. For example, the director of nursing provided updates on what constituted a quarantine and what constituted isolation. She walked them through contact-tracing protocols and what she learned from health experts on mitigation strategies like masking and social/physical distancing.

The district had so many decisions to make, and in its state, these decisions were all left to local school districts. One example was masks. The superintendent kept a list in his journal of the many considerations left to each district:

- Should we buy face shields?
- Do we need to buy masks for children?
- Should we require them? Encourage them? Strongly encourage them? Expect them?
- Will masks be worn indoors or outdoors? How do we avoid power struggles with kids who refuse to wear them?
- What about children with special needs? There are a multitude of reasons why kids won't wear them.
- What about kids who have suffered trauma?
- What about bullying for not wearing them? Or bullying for wearing them?
- What would a mask break look like at school?
- Should we require teachers to wear them? What is the NEA's official position?
- What are the other local school districts, colleges, and universities doing? Can we stand with our educational partners?
- What do parents and guardians think about this?

The last question prompted the school district to engage its families using two tools: a virtual webinar and an online platform for community feedback.

MASK WEBINAR

In May 2020, the stylists at a hair salon in Springfield, Missouri, tested positive for COVID-19. They had styled countless clients' hair before being diagnosed with the virus. Not one of their customers tested positive. Why was that? Masks. It was determined that the masks worn by the employees of the hair salon worked as an important mitigation strategy. This story as well as the emerging evidence about masks prompted the school district to consider requiring masks. The superintendent consulted pediatric infectious disease experts who all highly recommended masks and physical distancing wherever possible.

The problem many superintendents faced throughout the state and across the nation was that half of their communities opposed a mask mandate, preferring to make masks optional. The superintendent held a webinar for families. He made a short presentation about the case rates in their city and county and asked parents and guardians for their feedback about whether masks should be encouraged or required.

For more than three hours, parents and guardians gave feedback. He wrote down what they said:

- "Masks save lives, but there should be exceptions to the rule, reasonable exceptions."
- "'Strongly encourage' is the way to go, with prompting and using feedback, no discipline."
- "Keep schools open as long as possible. You need stakeholder satisfaction."
- "Exceptions may need to be considered. Be cognizant of the whole community."
- "I support 'encouraging' and not 'mandating.'"
- "I'm ready to send kids to school. My work schedule makes it difficult. Mandate the rules. School is a safe environment for kids."
- "Have you considered mandating middle and high schools and not elementary?"
- "I am strongly against requiring masks at school. Many will not feel safe wearing a mask. That'll make it or break it for us."
- "Encourage masks in the classrooms. I support mandating, but exceptions are needed."
- "Other countries in this world are mandating. Singapore, for example. Kids will adapt."
- "Clarify the expectation. Masks should be mandatory. Take mask breaks and do outside learning."
- "What supports will be put in place for children with special needs?"
- "Public health standards are clear. Perfect is the enemy of good."
- "I am in favor of masks and exceptions. I support face shields and up-to-date ventilation in every building."

- "I am concerned about making this mandatory. There are some health risks of wearing masks. For example, a false sense of security."
- "I am a teacher and a parent, and I support exemptions and think about harming other people's health. How horrifying it would be if someone got sick. We'd ask ourselves, 'did we do everything we could?'"
- "I don't have a strong decision. Masks do protect others. If schools close because they didn't require masks, then requiring masks would eliminate the need to close schools due to COVID-19 outbreaks."
- "I am strongly in favor of having masks. I have three kids in elementary. Ages two and older should wear masks. Many don't wear masks. Protect our kids!"
- "I support masks. Why would you allow exceptions? Why can't they wear masks? Make it part of the dress code."
- "Masks are saving lives."
- "Maybe compromise on elementary, giving them a special provision since they are in stable groups in their classrooms. They can wear masks in hallways when they come into contact with others."
- "What about teachers who work in multiple buildings? I am curious about whether they will transmit the virus from one building to another. You should also have high school students wipe down their surfaces and wear their masks."
- "We're a school system. We teach. We can build stamina. Make masks a part of their life."
- "We're underestimating what our kids can handle."
- "Exemptions for medical reasons only. Kids can do this. Make it fun and play it up."
- "Kindergartners and first graders can model mask wearing. Give kids a chance."
- "It will not be easy to enforce masks. What will you do if they don't follow the guidelines?"
- "Can masks be adjustable if they are not comfortable? Do they have to be worn on the bus, too?"
- "If masks are not mandatory, COVID-19 is more likely to spread."
- "You should survey parents and ask them what they want."
- "Explain to kids why we're wearing masks. Treat masks like a beginning-of-the-year routine."
- "Kids shouldn't wear masks because of speech and language concerns."
- "We should think smart and work smart. My daughter wants masks."
- "Enforcing masks is difficult, but let's try it. I support exceptions and mask breaks."
- "Decision making is hard when we don't know what the district is going to do."

- "We need to prioritize wearing masks and the health of the children and the greater community. Exemptions are appropriate."
- "My family wears masks (grades first and fourth), but elementary kids maybe have different needs. There may be long-term issues like misunderstanding social cues or carrying a larger viral load."

In addition to the webinar, the superintendent conducted a ThoughtExchange,[1] a tool to get a sense of what one's community is thinking. The way it works is you pose a question and participants are given an opportunity to provide a response. Once they submit their response, everyone else can rate the response on a five-point scale. This allows the entire community to see what ideas and thoughts resonate most. It is not a vote, but rather the ability to harvest the thoughts of a community. When you've concluded the process, you can see where groups of people agree or disagree. For example, this comment was equally supported by all groups: "Encourage and practice hygiene. It's common sense and is also educational for little people growing up." This comment was supported strongly by one group and opposed strongly by the other group: "CPS is being driven by fear which will fail us all. It is the job of educators to teach our children. Not to keep children healthy." The group that supported that comment strongly opposed the following comment: "Our children's safety is the most important thing to me and limiting their exposure to the COVID-19 virus as much as humanly possible. Limited exposure is important to keeping our children healthy and able to learn. The virus moves too quickly and infects many without proper precautions."

The superintendent reflected on the year. The year started with a compass and a declaration that the district was headed in the right direction, that it knew the way. It concluded with many more questions and no clear path.

WHAT GOT OVERLOOKED?

On August 21, 2018, the Great American Eclipse crossed the entire nation. For the first time in nearly a century, the United States experienced a total solar eclipse, starting in Oregon and concluding in South Carolina. The superintendent's community was in the direct line to experience the total solar eclipse. There was plenty of time to work with local and national astronomers to celebrate this cosmic event.

More than a year prior to this day, the district ordered eclipse glasses for every child and employee. Planned activities and events would culminate with coming outside to experience the eclipse. The schools communicated with parents and guardians and provided options for those who wanted to excuse their children from the experience. The administration communicated with principals and teachers and provided extra adult support at the early grades to ensure children could put their glasses on (and keep them on). They provided clear expectations. It was a wonderful day.

The weeks and days leading up to the Great American Eclipse included a lot of information for families along with requests for information and opinions. In this case, the information gathered helped the administration make decisions. The superintendent remarked how those decisions had been very different from the decisions they were making in 2020 when it came to COVID-19. A big difference, of course, was that astronomers could predict an eclipse, an astronomical event that happens at least twice a year. In the case of a global pandemic, the last one took place one hundred years prior. The only counsel that could be derived was from written records.

What got overlooked in all the communications the superintendent was facilitating was that many parents associated his information gathering with a referendum. They saw the ThoughtExchange tool, for example, as a vote. When his decisions or recommendations didn't reflect their beliefs, they decided that their voices were discounted and ignored. The superintendent overlooked the importance of making the process incredibly clear.

WHAT WAS LEARNED ABOUT RELATIONSHIPS?

When the superintendent was a classroom teacher, he invited a local musician to teach a song to his class. Mr. Kelly taught the students a song that would forever become his rallying song. With very simple lyrics, "We Are One" was a song focused on the commonalities we share as we grow up. As a teacher, he taught it to every class he ever had.

When he became an administrator, he taught it to the entire school. Every Monday, he gathered the entire school together to sing the song. He reminded the students and the staff to stand tall and to be proud of who they are and where they came from. He urged them to grow strong in body and mind and implored them to be kind to one another. "We Are One" meant that they had each other's backs and that they would never let each other down. It was a promise.

The superintendent often thought about the lyrics of this song and how firmly rooted they were in his mind, especially when he decided to reach out to the community at the beginning of the pandemic. When the pandemic hit in March 2020, he called on the community and the community called upon him.

They worked together to deliver food throughout the city so that every child had access to food. The county provided the necessary funds to purchase Wi-Fi hot spots for families so that they could access online learning. Organizations like the United Way, the local school foundation, and local businesses made sure school supplies and personal protection equipment were readily accessible at no cost. A local high school student asked to use the school district's 3D printer to coordinate the printing of thousands of face shields for first responders and essential personnel. Like the song he sang as a teacher and leader, the superintendent saw this as a "we are one" moment.

At the very beginning of the pandemic, the local community worked together. They were one. What started with everyone working together, with parades for teachers and "heroes work here" signs, soon became fractured relationships between friends and neighbors. School districts across the country were caught in the middle, navigating a no-win situation and looking to state and federal leaders to lead. What the superintendent learned was that relationships can be easy to gain but sometimes hard to sustain.

WHAT WAS FRUSTRATING?

When asked to think about what frustrated him during this point in the pandemic, the superintendent remarked, "So many decisions were left to me to make. I was getting so many opinions, suggestions, and demands. I didn't know what to do. It was almost paralyzing!"

This statement brings to mind the story of two men, a father and his son, walking their old horse to town to buy supplies. As they walked, the father invited his son to ride on the old horse. "There is no sense in us *both* walking to town," the father remarked. The two men happened upon a traveler walking from town who stopped to criticize the son for riding while his father walked. The son, feeling guilty, dismounted and invited his father to ride the horse. His father agreed and they continued their journey. After a short while, they met another traveler who criticized the father for riding the horse and making his son walk. "You should both ride the horse, for you will need your strength for the return trip." The father and son agreed, and the son mounted the horse to join his father.

The two men rode the old horse a bit further and met one last traveler on the outskirts of town. He said, "How cruel of you two to ride this poor old horse. Shame on you!" So what did the two men do? They dismounted and carried the horse to town!

From the very beginning of the pandemic, it seemed that the superintendent could satisfy no one. Every decision he made was with careful consideration and regular communication with experts in public health, epidemiology, infectious diseases, and virology. Their advice sometimes conflicted with the opinions of other medical professionals in the community and often conflicted with how state leaders approached the pandemic.

What was most frustrating was the lack of centralized leadership. The COVID-19 pandemic should not have been left entirely to local communities. There should have been statewide leadership making more than just "recommendations."

Interestingly, when school districts followed those state-level recommendations, they were then second-guessed and publicly reprimanded for following the advice of the virologists, pediatric infectious disease specialists, state officers of the American Academy of Pediatrics, and epidemiologists responsible for writing the state's pandemic plan. What was frustrating was the repeated public statement that local communities are unique, and one approach should not be the answer. What was frustrating was the inability to respect those words.

In the next chapter, the superintendent experiences an even more coordinated effort by the state legislature and attorney general to punish communities that followed the advice of the medical and scientific community.

WHAT COULD HAVE BEEN DONE DIFFERENTLY?

Every superintendent across the nation has wrestled with this question since the pandemic began. What could have been done differently? Superintendents regularly reached out to experts and engaged parents and guardians. They sought advice and counsel from internal stakeholders and leaders from every level. They regularly attended meetings hosted by state and national leaders. They convened superintendent focus groups to plan and problem solve. They spoke with their contemporaries in other states. What else could have been done?

Recently, the Waters Center for Systems Thinking introduced me to a concept called "accidental adversaries." Jennifer Kemeny described the idea of accidental adversaries by pointing out exactly what was being experienced by so many school and district leaders: "how partners can turn into bitter enemies when a win-win situation becomes unintentionally dominated by adversarial behavior." She continued:

"Accidental Adversaries" starts with two groups who have chosen to work together because they can mutually support each other's success. If the alliance works, both groups will gain increasing success. The problem arises when one or both parties is not satisfied with its current performance and takes corrective measures, which unintentionally obstruct the partner's success.[2]

I described this to the superintendent who, like me, wished he had known about this archetype earlier in his career. Perhaps by recognizing this conflict and working through it, he could have found a way back to a more symbiotic relationship. Although he was meeting with countless experts to guide his district's decisions, to some extent, he was shutting out some members of his own community.

At this point in the pandemic, he may have missed an opportunity to better engage with those who he knew loved their children and cared deeply for their community but who saw the situation through a completely different lens. Maybe, in the words of Margaret Wheatley, he needed to be more "willing to be disturbed." In her book *Turning to One Another: Simple Conversations to Restore Hope to the Future*, she wrote:

> As we work together to restore hope to the future, we need to include a new and strange ally—our willingness to be disturbed. Our willingness to have our beliefs and ideas challenged by what others think. No one person or perspective can give us the answers we need to the problems of today. Paradoxically, we can only find those answers by admitting we don't know. We have to be willing to let go of our certainty and expect ourselves to be confused for a time.[3]

The superintendent, reintroduced to Margaret Wheatley's wisdom, considered how he could have looked for additional ways to listen and to learn.

WHAT WAS SOMETHING GOOD THAT CAME OUT OF THIS EXPERIENCE?

When thinking about the good that came out of this difficult period, the superintendent was reminded of how much good there was. He wrote in his journal a note he would share over and over with his team: "The most amazing people work here. I'd like to see any district doing it better than we are."

At this point in the pandemic, with a prolonged closure looming, his team was linking arms with the community and mobilizing resources. They made sure Wi-Fi hot spots and technology were available. If families needed support, they personally visited homes or set up help desks in school parking lots all over the district.

They provided social and emotional support through their curriculum with face-to-face sessions and with telehealth through their school counselors and mental health outreach teams. They prepared and drove meals to nearly one hundred bus stops around town and provided grab-and-go meals at school sites. Teachers were doing online "tuck-in" lessons at night and reading bedtime stories to children.

They knew how the superintendent felt about the situation based on his conversations with the business community. They knew that he wanted to return to normal and that he wanted the community's economy and schools to open. They also knew the advice the district was getting meant instruction was going to continue to be virtual instruction so that they could protect families and friends from the pandemic.

The school year ended a few days after Minneapolis police officer Derek Chauvin killed George Floyd. The superintendent wrote the following note to all employees:

> When I first became a teacher, I met a veteran teacher named Marilyn Noble. Marilyn, originally from Southern California, moved to Northern California to attend UC Berkeley right at the beginning of the Free Speech Movement. Marilyn was a community organizer and a fighter for children and their families. Her students loved her, and their parents, many of whom sought advice and counsel navigating a system not designed for them, stood in awe of her fiery spirit. So did I. With her wooden cane in hand, she marched everywhere, always with purpose. To this day, I remain in touch with Marilyn. She is in her eighties and remains a beacon and sanctuary for so many. A few men, cast out by their families for identifying as members of the LGBTQ+ community, continue to find sanctuary in her home.
>
> Why do I bring up Marilyn on our last contracted day for teachers? Because today, a few days after George Floyd's death, she would have urged me to take the time to teach our students about their rights and about justice (and injustice). She would have invited me to her classroom to teach our combined classes songs about freedom. She would have insisted we all lean into the discomfort and honor one of the working assumptions of the district's equity work: "Oppression is destructive to the human spirit."
>
> COVID-19 will one day become inconsequential, but oppression (prejudice, discrimination, marginalization, powerlessness, exploitation, violence, and cultural imperialism) will remain. The Free Speech Movement launched a change in how people challenged the status quo. There will be a lot of changes in the new year. I, for one, would like to be a part of restoring love, compassion, empathy, and grace back into our world. If it can be done anywhere, it is in our school district.

The superintendent wished he could have said that the coming year would be easier. What was first proposed as a two-week stay-at-home order for districts across the nation had become more than two months. As we all know now, after the pandemic, the coming year would be anything but easy.

WATERS CENTER FOR SYSTEMS THINKING HABITS

A Leader Observes How Elements within Systems Change over Time, Generating Patterns and Trends
A Leader Considers Short-Term, Long-Term, and Unintended Consequences of Actions

Leaders must consider the types of trends or patterns that emerge over time. For the superintendent described in this chapter, trust in the system was strained while the district remained in remote learning. What were some things you noticed in your own organization? How did your decisions impact the organization? What were some unintended consequences of the decisions you made?

NOTES

1. "Enterprise Discussion Management," ThoughtExchange, https://thoughtexchange.com/ (accessed October 22, 2022).

2. "'Accidental Adversaries': When Friends Become Foes," The Systems Thinker, https://thesystemsthinker.com/accidental-adversaries-when-friends-become-foes/ (accessed October 22, 2022).

3. Margaret J. Wheatley, *Turning to One Another: Simple Conversations to Restore Hope to the Future* (San Francisco: Berrett-Koehler, 2002), 34.

Chapter 9

The Vision Is Clear?

How Their Systems Saved Them

There have been as many plagues as wars in history; yet always plagues and wars take people equally by surprise.

—Albert Camus, The Plague

What happened?
The global pandemic changed everything.
What got overlooked?
There are political ramifications for every decision.
What was learned about relationships?
Some of the most meaningful relationships are formed during crises.
What was frustrating?
The absence of empathy and compassion can divide a community.
What could have been done differently?
Publicly working through one's decision-making processes and being available promote trust.
What was something good that came out of this experience?
Systems saved, innovation emerged, and relationships deepened.

The Spanish word *arroyo* means "brook" (that is, a stream). Arroyo also happens to be the last name of the superintendent's dear friend, Julian. Throughout his life, Julian Arroyo has served as an inspiration. It's not because of his talents as a dancer and singer (although he has impressive talent in those areas), but rather because of the almost daily messages he puts out for the world consider. Whenever they are posted, the superintendent read

89

them as a way to "fuel up" and provide encouragement to others. Readers of this book will have pandemic stories that they will inevitably pass down to the generations that follow. One day, a message from Julian came across the superintendent's screen:

> "If we're not actually lifting each other up, then we're simply holding each other down."

Arroyo means "brook," and brooks sustain life. Julian Arroyo's messages helped sustain the superintendent during this time. They reminded him to seek ways to lift others up. In this chapter, he was tasked with doing just that.

Every winter, the Technology Services department would ask the superintendent for the coming year's theme. Staff would work on an image and then spend the summer uploading it to every electronic device in the school district. The year that he gave compasses to all the district's leaders coincided with an image of a compass and the phrase "We Know the Way" on more than twenty-five thousand school district devices.

In January 2020, the superintendent was asked for the coming year's motto. He thought it would be clever to use an image of glasses and to play on the idea of 20/20 vision being perfect vision. The motto would be "The Vision Is Clear!" Then the pandemic hit, and no one thought to reconsider this. No one even saw it until the beginning of the new school year.

Can you imagine what it looked like whenever *anyone* turned on a computer? The ridiculousness of it all? The monitor would click on and there it would be, "The Vision Is Clear!" Someone would walk past a computer lab and every one of those glowing monitors would read "The Vision Is Clear!" With the pandemic in full swing, the vision was most definitely not clear. It was murky at best.

WHAT HAPPENED?

In the coming sections, you're going to read about some horrifying things. The abuse the superintendent faced will be unsurprising for many of the leaders who read this book. Some leaders I talked to before writing this book had to hire personal security for themselves and their families. Some, pacifists by nature, bought their first firearms.

As the superintendent looked back on this year to deconstruct what frustrated him and what good came out of the experience, he had a lot to say. Thinking about the relationships that were formed was not hard because some of the most genuine and enduring relationships began during this time.

During this time, school districts around the nation continued to update and amend their pandemic plans. The superintendent was doing the same thing. The board of education delayed the beginning of the school year until after Labor Day. The school district created videos, hosted webinars, and generated visuals for parents so that they would know what a typical day would look like for virtual or hybrid learning (in which portions of the week would include in-seat learning and the rest of the week would be virtual). District staff continued to deliver meals to entire families, and they continued to mobilize the resources of the community to any family in need.

The coming year was a series of difficult decisions, all with the health and safety of the community as a driving force. The superintendent knew it was going to be an impossibly hard year. His final message to his leadership team, just days before the official start of the school year, stated:

> I wanted to start off this morning with a reminder of who we are as a team. We're a smart team, and a compassionate team. The COVID work has dominated every moment and will continue to do that throughout the foreseeable future. We are a connected team, too. And as we continue to serve the children and families of our community and as we continue to work to be the best employers for our employees, I want to say that I am so thankful to be doing this work with each of you.

WHAT GOT OVERLOOKED?

Throughout this book, the superintendent described in each chapter has learned a lot about the development of a leader. In his early years as superintendent, he struggled to harvest the wisdom of the organization as part of articulating a cohesive vision. He created too many goals and caused anxiety. He overlooked the power of creating reliable processes, which caused confusion and frustration.

When he first started as a leader, his communication style could have been described as one-way communication. It wasn't collaborative. He overlooked the importance of authentically sharing leadership. There is a difference between delegating responsibilities and sharing leadership. It took him a while to recognize and honor the difference. His experiences leading up to the pandemic prepared him to serve as a human-centered leader. Imperfect, certainly, but a leader who worked to learn deeply—the core of the model for human-centered school transformation. In looking back, thinking about what got overlooked was not easy.

When posed this question, the superintendent thought about how hard it was to navigate angry adults. As a principal and central office administrator, he always told people that when parents or guardians are yelling at you, they are mostly conveying their fear for their child. When a child has been suspended from school for the fourth time, they are not yelling at you because they hate you, they are yelling because they are scared, and they don't know what to do. That was the case during the pandemic. Parents were scared for their children, and they were seeking any possible answer that would lead them back to normal. The system always works aggressively toward the status quo. In this case, status quo was a return to what school looked like before the pandemic.

In thinking about what got overlooked, however, the superintendent overlooked how aggressively the system would work to return to stasis. He overlooked that while his experiences prepared him to lead his organization through a global pandemic, the pandemic was being used to further political ambitions that masqueraded as a promise of a return to normal.

He overlooked the fact that after decades of failed attempts to pass voucher and charter legislation, politicians and lobbyists were using parents and guardians to their advantage. When he responded to a question or a concern, his response was used to push for vouchers. If he didn't respond to an email, his silence was used to push for charter schools. He overlooked how calculated and intentional the campaign was.

WHAT RELATIONSHIPS WERE FORMED?

Superintendents serve on many community committees and nonprofit boards. It's part of their role. Their presence on these boards helps promote good communication and even better collaboration. These relationships capture the interconnectedness of society. For example, when a community has a conversation about homelessness, it's important to see how this one issue is tied to every entity throughout the community. The same for public schools. Public school districts are an organism dependent on everything else. Without relationships, they struggle. During the global pandemic, the meaningful connections within and between systems were essential.

With the pandemic ever present, the superintendent attended "COVID-19 and Kids" sessions sponsored by medical professionals.[1] This was a weekly meeting led by pediatricians, pediatric infectious disease specialists, nurses, psychologists, and public health directors. The sessions always included new learning followed by a case study.

One week, the session focused on compassion fatigue. Having a greater difficulty maintaining the same degree of empathy? Feeling mentally exhausted? Experiencing sleep disturbance? Feeling impatient or like a failure? As they reviewed all of these signs and symptoms of compassion fatigue, the superintendent had a jarring thought, "Oh my gosh, that's me!"

Throughout the year, the superintendent had been feeling powerless. He knew that everyone wanted to figure out the right formula for getting children back to school without interruption. He knew that everyone wanted to heal the wounds the pandemic had created between friends and neighbors. He knew that everyone was determined to do the very best for the children in the community, yet the emails, the phone calls, the news media, the insults at public meetings and on social media, the yard signs in traffic medians, and the police cars parked outside the homes of the superintendent and board of education members for months represented the worst in people.

As part of their learning that week in the "COVID-19 and Kids" session, there was a slide about healthy responses to compassion fatigue. They reminded the participants to make sure they were talking about this with others, to make sure they were finding activities that bring joy and help release endorphins, and to make sure they were reminding themselves of what they stood for, including their pre-pandemic goals.

When the superintendent looked back on what was learned about relationships, he was grateful for the incident command structure they created and maintained. He didn't know what he would have done had the brain trust not worked together to action plan and communicate essential information. There were occasional hijinks in this group as well. Leaving liquor on each other's doorsteps was not uncommon ("quantity over quality" was the note on a barrel of low-quality bourbon left on the superintendent's front steps). The local health department, under the leadership of a well-respected health director, contacted the superintendent daily to plan and process. The ongoing communication built a deep level of trust within and among the systems.

WHAT WAS FRUSTRATING?

All leaders carry other people's traumas with them. Employees experience loss and they look to their leaders for empathy. Children, many of them too young to make meaning of their trauma, look to the adults in their lives for physical and emotional safety. Leaders give every bit of themselves to help them, and often it feels as though giving their all is not enough.

One day, the superintendent woke to the news that one of the students for whom his system had cared so deeply had been accused of committing murder. He had known the young man since he was seven. From the moment he met him, the superintendent was impressed by his intelligence and charisma. He could see, too, that the boy was dealing with personal demons. He would write the most inspired narrative only to then lose it completely, requiring the classroom to be evacuated.

As a school district, they refused to run away from the boy. Instead, they leaned in. Everyone did. When he entered middle school, they fell in love with him, too. They saw his potential. When he went to three different high schools because of the continual trauma of being evicted from his home, the same love, compassion, and empathy was bestowed upon him and his family. A community mentor stuck with him through his high school graduation and regularly asked the superintendent what else she could do to help him. A highlight for the superintendent was when he was able to give him the biggest congratulatory hug, right there on the stage, at his high school graduation.

The world was his.
And now his life seemed to be over.

Close colleagues tried to comfort the superintendent. "Maybe his life isn't over. Maybe this is the beginning of a different path," one said. Another said, "Don't despair. We can't. Our kids need us." They were right. The superintendent was thankful to them for helping him dust off his knees and get back in the game. He would look back on this experience as he continued navigating the school district through a global pandemic, an almost impossible task. He would look back on this experience and do his very best to practice empathy and grace, even though there were so many in the community and throughout the state unable to do the same.

THE RETURN TO IN-SEAT LEARNING

In October, the superintendent made a recommendation and the board approved a plan to bring elementary students back for in-seat learning. They made the recommendation based on conversations with the health department and infectious disease specialists and the feedback they were hearing from parents, guardians, and teachers. After the first week, despite quarantining more than one hundred people, including principals, teachers, and children, the reports had been mostly positive.

Even though middle and high school students continued to join the more than two hundred thousand students statewide in an all-virtual model, they also used the October date to resume in-person special education programming at the middle schools (they held in-person classes for self-contained pre-K–12 special education classrooms from the very beginning of the school year).

Throughout this time, the middle schools and high schools were working aggressively to find ways to help struggling students. They created systems to make sure supplies were being delivered. They had counselors and outreach support regularly making home visits. They had teachers teaching students on front porches. When the following claims were made in person, at board meetings, or on social media, they really had to dig deep and simply provide the truth.

SUNSHINE REQUESTS

The school district was being overwhelmed by open records requests for all emails between leaders, the board of education, and the city/county health department. A claim was made that the district had charged thousands of dollars to process a single request. They would never charge such a fee for Sunshine Requests, but when the request asked for fifty million emails, it would have required additional staff to process. So the school district called the individual and asked if he would narrow his search. He did, and they processed it for a nominal fee.

SPECIAL EDUCATION SERVICES

A claim was made that the school district was not providing special education services. The claim was that the board of education voted to deny students individualized education program services. This was not true. Even before the Department of Elementary and Secondary Education released guidelines, the school district was looking for ways to bring back children with disabilities. Districtwide classrooms, for example, returned on September 8, the very first day of the school year.

Additionally, the school district created on-demand video tutorials on a specially designed parent and community website. In an email to staff, the superintendent wrote, "We all agree we want to get all of our children back in school, both here in our community and throughout the state. We know everyone is exhausted trying to juggle parenting, working, and school. We all want to be back to normal. The problem is that there is nothing normal about a global pandemic. But I promise you we will continue to listen." A few days later, the school district was summoned to a Joint Hearing of the State Senate and House of Representatives.

JOINT COMMITTEE ON EDUCATION

On October 24, the Joint Committee on Education, a committee of state senators and representatives, held a committee hearing next door to the superintendent's office to discuss COVID-19.[2] This was highly unusual since committee
hearings were typically conducted at the Capitol Building. In this case, with
the town's proximity to the capital and with access to multiple media outlets,
the more than five-hour hearing was held in the superintendent's community.

On her website describing the hearing, the senator, a self-described cham-
pion for charter schools, said, "It is important for state leaders, school officials, parents and students to come together and have their voices heard on
this important issue." In what could only be described as a public execution
of public education, the superintendent was instructed to sit in the front row
while preselected parents and children gave public testimony about the dif-
ficulties they were having with virtual learning.

After each testimonial, participants were asked whether they would accept
a voucher if it were made available to them. Many responded that they would.
At some point in the hearing, the board president, another board of education
member, and the superintendent were invited to make a statement and answer
questions. The superintendent said:

> Good afternoon and thank you for this invitation. I know I can speak for the
> board members here by saying we very much appreciate being included in
> statewide education discussions like this one. I think it is so appropriate that you
> chose to hold this Joint Committee meeting in our community. Our town, in so
> many ways, is a microcosm of the state. It is urban, it is suburban, and it is rural.
>
> In March, April, May, and June, our community's data looked promising. We
> were having fewer than ten cases per day, and we released an initial survey. I say
> "initial" because many in our community remind me regularly that 80 percent of
> the community voted for in-person, and they did! That is, until our local cases of
> COVID-19 changed, and our families changed their minds, too.
>
> Senator, it would be like a family voting to travel for its family reunion. Let's
> say 80 percent chose a beach vacation and 20 percent chose to go an amusement
> park. But when a hurricane was projected to hit the very beach the family chose,
> the family matriarch said, "We really need to rethink heading to the beach." It
> would seem inappropriate if the members of the family protested, if they said,
> "But 80 percent of us want to go to the beach. We voted!" You have to use the
> data you have in front of you to make the very best decision you can.
>
> I am not an epidemiologist. I am not a virologist. I am not a pediatric infec-
> tious disease doctor. I am not a pediatrician. And I am not a public health direc-
> tor with years and years of experience. What I *am* is a teacher—and the CEO of
> the third-largest employer in this community. In those two roles, I have an obli-
> gation to the nineteen thousand children and three thousand employees to keep

them safe. That's my first job. And because my background is in literacy and second language learning, I do what any leader does: I reached out to all of those experts who could provide advice and counsel. I also reached out to 4,500 parents who provided more than 212,000 responses to more than 7,000 comments.

What we learned was our community is split. Again, it's a microcosm of the state. It's not surprising that after all the comments and responses, we reached common ground on this: the highest priority was for the safety of children, staff, and the community.

We listened.

We heard.

We acted.

Our decisions have been, and will continue to be, evidence based.

Throughout his entire testimony, the superintendent looked up from time to time to see many of the legislators looking at their phones. They appeared to be disinterested in what he had to say. The only conclusion he could reach was that they didn't care about what he had to say. That was frustrating.

When one of the senators, in defiance of the local health department's mask mandate, said he had a question, the superintendent quickly jumped in and said, "Senator, if it is to ask me if I would accept a voucher, I would not." When asked if he regretted succumbing to impulsivity, he said he regretted making the joke but found it amusing that the senator laughed (as did many in the room). The ridiculousness of it all was so incredibly frustrating.

The superintendent was observing local control being forced to take a back seat to a statewide effort to downplay the seriousness of the pandemic so that vouchers and charter school legislation could finally become law.

I GIVE THEM A BIG FAT "F"

In January, a locally elected state representative rated the school district an "F" during a committee hearing debating the reallocation of funding away from school districts teaching in a virtual platform.[3] The superintendent wrote her a letter and published it in the local newspaper. He wrote:

Dear Representative:

There was once a time when civility prevailed. There was once a time when local delegates stood up for their community. Locally elected officials would publicly support and privately question or criticize. I am flabbergasted and flummoxed by your public statement that our school district is an "F."

Our district is one of the highest performing school districts in the state. Our district is annually recognized for budgeting excellence. Our teachers, our leaders, and our students are regularly recognized on a state and national level. Our students regularly outperform their state, national, and international peers on the ACT and every advanced placement exam. More than 90 percent of our graduates enlist in the military, enter the workforce, or attend two- or four-year colleges.

When you say the district is an "F," you are saying our community, the community you represent, is an "F." You are saying the good people in our community who elected you are an "F." That is false. As a public servant, you serve as a role model to the students in our district. You just modeled that name-calling and attempts at public shaming are what responsible adults and leaders should do. That is the antithesis of all the antibullying efforts we promote daily.

As a model for our next generation, please remember that they remember what you say and how you make them feel. Civility. During this period in history, we must return to that. Be the critical friend we need you to be.

WHAT COULD HAVE BEEN DONE DIFFERENTLY?

A month before he wrote that letter, the superintendent wrote a note in his journal. He had just read an article about mochi making in Kyoto, Japan.[4] He wrote:

> For more than one thousand years (seventy generations), they have operated the same business. We're being asked to do something well for ten months without the constant disruption of a new model. We're getting better each day. Virtual is going so much more smoothly now and it will continue to improve. I've been so impressed with our teachers and how well it's going. Virtual school is working and gives everyone consistency, which may be one of the most important determining factors.

When he looked back on this entry, he thought to himself whether he could have done a better job of considering Margaret Wheatley's advice from the previous chapter: to allow oneself to be disturbed. By this point, he had made his mind up that they were going to provide the best version of the model they were doing rather than jumping from one model to the next, something that he felt would be a major disruption for families.

While the district's team walked through a "look, listen, learn, lead" process whenever it was presented with an idea, the superintendent reflected on what he could have done differently. He concluded he could have publicly walked through that process so that it didn't appear as though he was dismissing the idea without consideration. It might have led him to conclude that returning sooner would have been responsive to the mental health needs of the district's children.

Additionally, he could have considered the Waters Center for System Thinking and a question about leverage it poses: Where might a small change have a long-lasting desired effect?[5] By doing these things, he could have built trust with those who felt sidelined.

WHAT WAS SOMETHING GOOD THAT CAME OUT OF THIS EXPERIENCE?

Daniel Mendelsohn's *An Odyssey: A Father, a Son, and an Epic*[6] is part memoir and part retelling of Homer's *Odyssey*. I don't typically become too emotionally involved in what I read, but there were times when I wept thinking about Telemachus searching for answers about his father. (And, by the way, how cool is it that the etymological roots of the word *mentor* came from one of Odysseus's closest friends and confidantes, whose name was Mentor?)

I'm not totally sure why I started to cry. It's possible because of my relationship to my own father, a hero to me, who lives far away and had been physically far away during the entire pandemic. The book made me think of the superintendent and his odyssey.

Maybe, like Odysseus, the superintendent had been stranded for what had felt like ten years. The promise of a vaccine appeared to be a promise to a return home, a sense of stability. There were several good things that came out of the pandemic. Although the superintendent was unsuccessful in bridging the ideological chasm that existed, he was proud of a few achievements.

THEIR SYSTEMS SAVED THEM

In November, the superintendent had a phone conversation with the health department director. She shared an interesting timeline direct from the community's archives:

In September 1918, twenty cases of the Spanish flu were identified.
In October, the mayor closed down the city.
In November, the community objected to the closings and raised additional objections to rules that masks be worn, so the mayor reopened the city.
In December, cases of the Spanish flu jumped, and the city was closed again. Additional regulations were introduced. No more than six people could gather in the same place.

The superintendent's response to her was, "I wonder if we can learn from history!" Throughout the pandemic, the district's systems were strong. They made decisions collaboratively and shared leadership without hesitation. They practiced empathy and compassion, and they lived their values conscientiously. As a team and with their partners, they practiced positive connectedness and did their best to remain patient and willing to learn from mistakes. Their systems saved them.

JAPAN CONNECTION

The year before the pandemic, the Nagano Prefecture formally invited the superintendent's school district to participate in Japan's National High School Culture Festival. They were asked to bring something quintessentially American. Initially, they proposed a jazz band, but the director of fine arts challenged the superintendent to approach this through a lens of access. What would be something quintessentially American and provide access to a large group of children? A drumline!

Percussion United, comprised of twenty student percussionists from the school district's three comprehensive high schools, traveled abroad to Japan to perform in the forty-second National High School Culture Festival in the city of Matsumoto. They were joined by other instrumental ensembles from Austria, South Korea, and China, as well as several Japanese marching bands in the 1998 Winter Olympics stadium.

The superintendent was given an opportunity to address a few hundred performers and their families. He thanked them for the invitation and said, "For so many, the world has been turned upside down, but this trip gives me hope that we can still build bridges of friendship and trust."

While in Nagano, the superintendent was introduced to his community's sister city in Hakusan, a few hours away by train. There he learned of the thirty-year relationship between the two cities and how 9/11 abruptly paused continued exchanges. It was there he began to dream of a restored relationship, with his district's children traveling annually to their STEM high school constructed at the base of Mount Hakusan.

The following year, just a few months before the pandemic changed everything, the superintendent sponsored a delegation representing the community's local colleges and university, the school district, city and county representatives, and chamber of commerce members. Together they celebrated the long relationship and made a formal commitment to restart sister city cultural exchanges, with the STEM high school serving as a focal point. Experiential learning in one of Japan's sacred mountains would be an unforgettable experience for the school district's children.

Although the pandemic caused a delay in starting the exchanges, the superintendent remained in contact with the Hakusan community. It helped him remain hopeful during a very dark time.

THE NATURE SCHOOL

From the initial days of the pandemic and during the height of it, the community overwhelmingly found common ground through the concept of creating outdoor learning opportunities for children. During the previous two years, they followed the superintendent's caterpillar, chrysalis, and butterfly process as well as the look, learn, listen, lead protocols while launching an innovative educational opportunity with the state's Department of Conservation.

Together, they would create a nature school.

The idea was to expand place-based learning opportunities for children. "Place based," as the superintendent would define it, was the belief that learning should not be confined to the four walls of a classroom. The district already practiced this philosophy on annual trips in which more than a thousand children would travel to either the Grand Tetons or the Great Smoky Mountains National Park. With this unique curriculum, kids would learn outdoors about the natural resources in their community through the lens of the environment, culture, and economics.

The learning would use existing district and state educational standards to take students on an exploratory journey into how their community operated and sustained itself. The project would be a partnership between the school district, the Department of Conservation, and the community.

Additionally, in the spirit of what they had learned about interconnectedness, they decided this project should provide placed-based educational opportunities for students in all of the county's school districts.

Throughout the pandemic, the superintendent collaborated regularly with the surrounding school districts, all small, rural districts. He came to realize that the many resources available in his district should be shared with those districts as well. He felt the nature school should be no different.

When completed, it would feature a school building of more than eight thousand square feet, with four classrooms and a wet lab (doubling as natural disaster shelter), lobby with educational displays, and sustainable design features to conserve water and energy. The building would reach more than twenty thousand students annually from all six of the county's school districts, including public, private, parochial, and home-school programs. This would include:

- twenty-two hundred fifth graders for an immersive seven-day experience connected back to their community school curriculum;
- sixteen thousand students from all grade levels for one-day field trips during warm months of the school year; and
- two thousand children and families during evening, weekend, and summer programming sponsored by the Department of Conservation and the city's Department of Parks and Recreation.

As of the writing of this book, the two-hundred-plus acre campus had opened officially. Students were camping, hiking, fishing, and exploring the property. A pavilion had been completed and the construction of the nature school building had begun.

ENDURING RELATIONSHIPS BUILT

The nature school was a direct result of the enduring relationships built on the very values the superintendent had established collaboratively. Those relationships existed before the pandemic and continued throughout it. The most notable relationships built as a result of the pandemic were the connections made with the health department and the "COVID-19 and Kids" sessions. The experts associated with these two networks became the superintendent's daily source of information and support and his sounding boards and emotional counselors.

Finally, internally, the superintendent was incredibly lucky to have had a smart and healthy cabinet, a selfless incident command team, and a supportive board of education.

Earlier, the superintendent mentioned the brain trust and its penchant for humor. For the final one hundred days of the school year, its members designed and created a one-of-a-kind tear-away calendar for the superintendent, which included pandemic phrases that became inside jokes that only the team understood. When everything else felt like it was spiraling out of control, these daily jokes anchored the superintendent and reminded him of his bond with the team. He shared a few of these phrases:

Bubble of trust—First and foremost, the brain trust worked because members trusted that whatever was said—however it was said—would remain in a bubble of trust.

Where's the link?—Despite being in Zoom meetings six hours a day for two years, they still couldn't figure out who was the host and who had the link.

You're muted—Even with all those Zooms, they still couldn't figure out how to unmute themselves!

I have one minute to pee before incident command—Back-to-back-to-back Zoom meetings are never a good idea. Apparently, the superintendent announced his need to go to the bathroom at the end of nearly every brain trust meeting. Talk about being comfortable with the team!

High hurdle—The superintendent gave multiple public pandemic updates each month. At every single update, he was asked by a board of education member if a specific idea (for example, what if half of the nineteen thousand students came to school in the morning and the other half came in the afternoon?) would be impossible or a "high hurdle." The brain trust chided the superintendent for not just saying impossible.

Chicken head—During public comment at one board of education meeting, a parent went to the podium and announced that if she were married to the superintendent, she would divorce him. She called the district a bunch of chickens and then put on a huge chicken head and walked out.

Dumpster fire—The superintendent regularly texted with superintendents from all over the state and nation. Members usually sent a picture or a meme to communicate their current situation to the group. The most frequently used image was that of a garbage dumpster on fire.

Monitoring . . . monitoring . . . monitoring—The brain trust made fun of the superintendent for repeatedly saying that he was "monitoring" situations. He didn't know what else to say! "What will you do when cases drop below the line you set for a return to in-seat learning?" "We are monitoring the case rates closely." His response was that he was "monitoring" because he was!

Poop doctor—Dr. Marc Johnson, professor of molecular microbiology and immunology at the University of Missouri, was advising multiple states and municipalities throughout the nation.[7] The superintendent routinely contacted Dr. Johnson. He was a valuable resource throughout the pandemic. The brain trust always wanted to know the predictions of the "poop doctor."

We DO have a plan!—Every meeting the school district held and every email it sent referenced its seventy-six-page pandemic plan. Without fail, though, community members went to the podium and accused the school district of not having a plan.

"The Vision Is Clear" (ha!)—One of the last messages of the year was probably the superintendent's favorite. He had no idea how inaccurate (and comical) his choice for a motto would be during a pandemic. It still makes him put his hands over his face, shake his head, and chuckle!

WATERS CENTER FOR SYSTEMS
THINKING HABITS

**A Leader Makes Meaningful Connections within
and between Systems
A Leader Uses Understanding of System Structure
to Identify Possible Leverage Actions**

Looking back, the superintendent reflected on how the school system was impacted by other systems (legislative, economic, and social systems). In thinking about your organization's relationship to other systems, how does the understanding of one system transfer to the understanding of another system?

Additionally, the superintendent observed how small changes could have improved outcomes. In your own work, are there small changes that you have not yet considered that could bring about desired results?

NOTES

1. "Show Me Strong Kids," Show-Me ECHO, https://showmeecho.org/clinics/covid-19-kids/ (accessed October 25, 2022).

2. "Senator Cindy O'Laughlin to Hold a Joint Committee on Education Hearing to Discuss the Effects of COVID-19 School Building Closures on Students and Parents," Missouri Senate, www.senate.mo.gov/20web/senator-cindy-olaughlin-to-hold-a-joint-committee-on-education-hearing-to-discuss-the-effects-of-covid-19-school-building-closures-on-students-and-parents/ (accessed October 25, 2022).

3. Wicker Perlis, "Fight Looms over Effort to Create Scholarships for Public School Students to Attend Private Schools," *Columbia Missourian*, January 26, 2021.

4. Ben Dooley and Hisako Ueno, "This Japanese Shop Is 1,020 Years Old. It Knows a Bit about Surviving Crises," *New York Times*, www.nytimes.com/2020/12/02/business/japan-old-companies.html (accessed October 22, 2022).

5. "Waters Center for Systems Thinking," Waters Center for Systems Thinking, https://thinkingtoolsstudio.waterscenterst.org/cards (accessed October 21, 2022).

6. Daniel Adam Mendelsohn, *An Odyssey: A Father, a Son, and an Epic* (New York: Vintage Books, 2018).

7. Emily Anthes, "From the Wastewater Drain, Solid Pandemic Data," *New York Times*, May 7, 2021.

Epilogue

L'instant de la decision est une folie. (The instant of decision is madness.)

—Kierkegaard

"WHY DO WE HAVE BOWLS WITH HOLES?!"

Who would ask such a question? Well, let me explain. Martin D. Ginsburg was my uncle. In his own right, he was an incredibly successful tax attorney and Georgetown Law School professor. He married his college sweetheart, Ruth Bader, who said Martin "was the first boy I met who cared I had a brain." In their house, Ruth would become Supreme Court Justice Ruth Bader Ginsburg and Marty would be known for both his intelligence and his recipes. In their house, as my cousin Jane once remarked, "My father did the cooking, and my mother did the thinking."

During one of the last conversations I had with my Uncle Martin before his death, we talked about food and how he influenced me to cook. He asked me whether my three boys were cooking at all. I tried a few times to have them help me in the kitchen, but it was not a regular occurrence. So I remember returning home from that visit and insisting that the boys make Saturday breakfast. Specifically, waffles. Our three boys treated the project differently.

Saturday morning arrived and the three boys went into the kitchen. Our oldest found the best recipe for waffles. Overnight waffles. Logical as he was, he shut the cookbook and declared that overnight waffles could not be made the same morning and promptly left the room. The other two were undeterred. They found a waffle recipe and set out to make waffles. Our second child was more like me, ready to act, sometimes without fully thinking things through. He started working on the waffles. The youngest child was more deliberate in his actions. He carefully assembled all the ingredients, measured them out, and rearranged their positions on the counter (at the rate he was moving, he seemed to be setting himself up for Sunday breakfast).

And then a scream erupted! My wife and I ran to the kitchen only to find a mess of waffle batter all over the counter. Our second son, in his haste, had grabbed a bowl for the dry ingredients and another bowl for the wet ingredients. He mixed them together only to find the mixture was oozing all over the place. He screamed, "Why do we have bowls with holes in them?!"

He had used a colander.

The children's approaches in the waffle story—with one who wouldn't even begin because the best couldn't be achieved, another carefully measuring and preparing endlessly, and the final one jumping right in—are entertaining. It is also a story to consider when you're thinking about leadership, systems thinking, and after-action reviews. It speaks to the different approaches we all take when it comes to situations and the lessons learned before, during, and after an event. It speaks to the imperfection of leadership. Anyone in leadership is an imperfect leader.

A few months later, my cousin Jane represented the family in the renaming of the Brooklyn Municipal Building, forever to be known as the Justice Ruth Bader Ginsburg Municipal Building.[1] New York City's mayor opened the brief ceremony and said something that really captured my attention. He said Ruth Bader Ginsburg "envisioned a different and better society" and worked tirelessly "to bring that vision to realization." That in itself was worth noting, but not necessarily noteworthy.

It was the listing of her credentials as a native Brooklynite that made me want to mention it here. As a child, she attended P.S. 238 and then James Madison High School. Her foundation was public education. My cousin Jane then continued that thread by saying her mother "was a proud graduate of public schools and regularly visited the Brooklyn Public Library." These institutions gave her the opportunity to think critically about the world. It was public education that served as a platform for her awakening to social injustices. My cousin recounted one such moment.

When Ruth was fourteen, the local youth orchestra, under the direction of Dean Dixon, "deepened her love of music."[2] Dean Dixon was African American and, in 1947 through 1948, faced a racially motivated movement forcing him to leave the United States for Europe (which he called home for the rest of his life). Ruth's takeaway from this event was "how prejudice deprives everyone of the talents it stifles."[3] I quickly jotted a note to myself: public education is the great equalizer. We cannot deny we've come so far and still there is so much more to do.

In fact, I was reminded of a quote from a speech my aunt once sent me. Justice Ginsburg wrote:

In the open society that is the American ideal, no doors should be closed to people willing to spend hours of effort needed to make dreams come true. So, hold fast to your dreams, and work hard to make them a reality. And as you pursue your paths in life, leave tracks. Just as others have been way pavers for you, so you should aid those who will follow in your way. Do your part to help move society to the place you would like it to be for the health and well-being of generations following your own.[4]

She borrowed a line from Langston Hughes, but she also captured how I felt about the future of public education. Education in America will never be the same. The decisions we make now and the ability to reach our kids in a meaningful way will be our contribution to the generation that follows us. We must keep working to make things better for all, not just some.

FINAL WORDS

The title of this book is *An Imperfect Leader: Human-Centered Leadership in (After) Action*. As I have learned from interviewing superintendents from all over the nation—and as we have learned from the experiences of the superintendent in this book—there is no such thing as a perfect leader. Most of us take on leadership roles, fight off daily bouts of imposter syndrome, and do the very best we can to bring people together to take meaningful steps forward.

Regardless of the industry, we wake up every day with the intent to do good and leave the world a little bit better than it was the previous day. Imperfect leadership is not a scarlet letter. It's a badge of honor. It recognizes that serving as a lead learner is about being a vulnerable leader, an empathetic leader, a compassionate leader.

I'm proud to be an imperfect leader. I'll keep looking at situations and considering what was overlooked and what relationships were made. I will continue to consider the frustrating moments and think about what could have been done differently. I will remain committed to looking at the good that came out of a situation. It's what imperfect leaders do.

NOTE

1. "Mayor Bill de Blasio Delivers Remarks at Renaming Ceremony in Honor of Justice Ruth Bader Ginsburg," YouTube, www.youtube.com/watch?v=XoSUEdW7NUI (accessed October 25, 2022).

2. Ibid.

3. Ibid.

4. "Baccalaureate Address by Supreme Court Justice Ruth Bader Ginsburg," https://www.brown.edu/Administration/News_Bureau/2001-02/01-142t.html (accessed February 1, 2023).

Bibliography

"A Model for Human-Centered School Transformation." Santa Fe Center for Transformational School Leadership. https://transformationalschoolleadership .com/transformation-leadership/model-for-human-centered-school-transformation. Accessed October 21, 2022.

AASA, the School Superintendents Association. www.aasa.org/home/. Accessed October 22, 2022.

"'Accidental Adversaries': When Friends Become Foes." The Systems Thinker. https://thesystemsthinker.com/accidental-adversaries-when-friends-become-foes/. Accessed October 22, 2022.

"After-Action Review." Wikipedia. https://en.wikipedia.org/wiki/After-action_ review. Accessed October 11, 2022.

Anderson, Gary L., Kathryn Herr, and Ann Sigrid Nihlen. *Studying Your Own School: An Educator's Guide to Practitioner Action Research.* Thousand Oaks, CA: Corwin Press, 1994.

Anthes, Emily. "From the Wastewater Drain, Solid Pandemic Data." *New York Times*, May 7, 2021.

"AVID/Closing the Achievement Gap in Education." Advancement via Individual Determination. www.avid.org/. Accessed October 22, 2022.

Brown, Juanita, and David Isaacs. *The World Café: Shaping Our Futures through Conversations That Matter.* San Francisco: Berrett-Koehler, 2006.

Bolman, Lee G., and Terrence E. Deal. *Reframing Organizations: Artistry, Choice, and Leadership.* Hoboken, NJ: Jossey-Bass, 1997.

Boulud, Daniel. *Letters to a Young Chef.* New York: Basic Books, 2017.

Chang, Margaret Scrogin, and Raymond Chang. *The Beggar's Magic.* New York: M. K. McElderry Books, 1997.

Cummins, Jim. "Pedagogies of Choice: Challenging Coercive Relations of Power in Classrooms and Communities." *International Journal of Bilingual Education and Bilingualism* 12, no. 3 (2009): 261–71. https://doi.org/10.1080 /13670050903003751.

Dooley, Ben, and Hisako Ueno. "This Japanese Shop Is 1,020 Years Old. It Knows a Bit about Surviving Crises." *New York Times*, December 2, 2020. www.nytimes .com/2020/12/02/business/japan-old-companies.html.

Dweck, Carol S. *Mindset: How You Can Fulfil Your Potential*. London: Robinson, 2012.

Ellis, Deborah. *The Breadwinner*. Toronto: Douglas & McIntyre, 2001.

"Enterprise Discussion Management." ThoughtExchange. https://thoughtexchange.com/. Accessed October 22, 2022.

"FaciliTrainer Certification Program (FTCP)." NCCJ St. Louis. www.nccjstl.org/ftcp. Accessed October 23, 2022.

Gafke, Roger A. *A History of Public School Education in Columbia*. Columbia, MO: Public School District, 1978.

Giono, Jean. *The Man Who Planted Trees*. New York: Random House, 2015.

"Habits of a Systems Thinker." Thinking Tools Studio, https://thinkingtoolsstudio.waterscenterst.org/cards. Accessed October 23, 2022.

Hart, Betty, and Todd R. Risley. *Meaningful Differences in the Everyday Experience of Young American Children*. Baltimore: Brookes, 1995.

Henke, Linda. *Leaders' Learning Work: The Language of Vision*. St. Louis, MO: Washington University Institute for School Partnership, 2017.

Hermann, Mary B. *Learn to Lead, Lead to Learn*. Lanham, MD: Rowman & Littlefield, 2019.

Hernandez, Paul. "Baldrige Performance Excellence Program." NIST. Last modified April 11, 2019. www.nist.gov/baldrige.

Herrick, E. "Prison Literacy Connection." *Corrections Compendium* 16, no. 12 (1991): 1, 5–9.

Kelly, Sean, and Heather Price. "The Correlates of Tracking Policy." *American Educational Research Journal* 48, no. 3 (2011): 560–85. https://doi.org/10.3102/0002831210395927.

Lambert, Linda. *Leaders as Lead Learners*. Santa Fe, NM: Santa Fe Center for Transformational School Leadership, 2019.

———. "Leadership Redefined: An Evocative Context for Teacher Leadership." *School Leadership & Management* 23, no. 4 (2013): 421–30.

Landowne, Youme. *Sélavi, That Is Life*. El Paso, TX: Cinco Puntos Press, 2005.

Lencioni, Patrick M. *The Advantage*. Hoboken, NJ: John Wiley, 2012.

Lynch, Matthew. 2014. "High School Dropout Rate: Causes and Costs." *HuffPost*, May 30, 2014. www.huffpost.com/entry/high-school-dropout-rate_b_5421778. Accessed October 22, 2022.

"Mayor Bill de Blasio Delivers Remarks at Renaming Ceremony in Honor of Justice Ruth Bader Ginsburg." YouTube. www.youtube.com/watch?v=XoSUEdW7NUI. Accessed October 25, 2022.

Mendelsohn, Daniel Adam. *An Odyssey: A Father, a Son, and an Epic*. New York: Vintage, 2018.

Mischel, Walter, and Ebbe B. Ebbesen. "Attention in Delay of Gratification." *Journal of Personality and Social Psychology* 16, no. 2 (1970): 329–37. https://doi.org/10.1037/h0029815.

"MSAN Network." Minority Student Achievement Network. http://msan.wceruw.org. Accessed October 21, 2022.

Muhammad, Anthony. *Transforming School Culture: How to Overcome Staff Division*. Bloomington, IN: Solution Tree Press, 2018.

National Summer Learning Association. "NBC's Brian Williams on Summer Learning Loss." YouTube. www.youtube.com/watch?v=M2haD7FhMys. Accessed October 23, 2022.

"Our Approach." Transformational Leadership Initiative. https://cpb-us-w2.wpmucdn .com/sites.wustl.edu/dist/7/2590/files/2018/05/twoPager_021618-153jco2.pdf. Accessed October 23, 2022.

Perlis, Wicker. "Fight Looms over Effort to Create Scholarships for Public School Students to Attend Private Schools." *Columbia Missourian*, January 26, 2021. www.columbiamissourian.com/news/state_news/fight-looms-over-effort-to -create-scholarships-for-public-school-students-to-attend-private-schools/article _b4e80584-5ff0-11eb-b9e7-2b11d7c8a5c3.html.

Putnam, Robert D. *Our Kids: The American Dream in Crisis*. New York: Simon & Schuster, 2016.

Reeves, Douglas B. "The Case against the Zero." *Phi Delta Kappan* 86, no. 4 (2004): 324–25. https://doi.org/10.1177/003172170408600418.

Rothstein, Richard. "The Racial Achievement Gap, Segregated Schools, and Segregated Neighborhoods: A Constitutional Insult." *Race and Social Problems* 7, no. 1 (2014): 21–30. https://doi.org/10.1007/s12552-014-9134-1.

Saxler, Patricia Kasak. "The Marshmallow Test: Delay of Gratification and Independent Rule Compliance." PhD diss., Harvard Graduate School of Education, 2016. https://dash.harvard.edu/handle/1/27112705.

"Senator Cindy O'Laughlin to Hold a Joint Committee on Education Hearing to Discuss the Effects of COVID-19 School Building Closures on Students and Parents." Missouri Senate. www.senate.mo.gov/20web/senator-cindy-olaughlin-to -hold-a-joint-committee-on-education-hearing-to-discuss-the-effects-of-covid-19 -school-building-closures-on-students-and-parents/. Accessed October 25, 2022.

Senge, Peter M. *The Fifth Discipline: The Art and Practice of the Learning Organization*. London: Random House Business, 2006.

"Show Me Strong Kids." Show-Me ECHO. https://showmeecho.org/clinics/covid-19 -kids/. Accessed October 25, 2022.

Stavros, Jacqueline M., Lindsey N. Godwin, and David L. Cooperrider. "Appreciative Inquiry." In *Practicing Organization Development*, ed. William J. Rothwell, Jackie Stavros, and Roland L. Sullivan, 96–116. Hoboken, NJ: John Wiley, 2015. https:// doi.org/10.1002/9781119176626.ch6.

"The Best and Worst Places to Grow Up: How Your Area Compares." *New York Times*, May 4, 2015. www.nytimes.com/interactive/2015/05/03/upshot/the-best -and-worst-places-to-grow-up-how-your-area-compares.html.

"Thinking Tools Studio." Waters Center for Systems Thinking. https:// thinkingtoolsstudio.waterscenterst.org/cards. Accessed October 21, 2022.

Townsend, Rene S., Gloria L. Johnston, Gwen E. Gross, Peggy Lynch, Lorraine Garcy, Benita Roberts, and Patricia B. Novotney. *Effective Superintendent-School Board Practices*. Thousand Oaks, CA: Corwin Press, 2006.

Waters Center for Systems Thinking. https://waterscenterst.org/. Accessed October 22, 2022.

"What Is Restorative Practices?" International Institute for Restorative Practices. www.iirp.edu/restorative-practices/what-is-restorative-practices. Accessed October 22, 2022.

Wheatley, Margaret J. *Turning to One Another: Simple Conversations to Restore Hope to the Future*. San Francisco: Berrett-Koehler, 2002.

Index

About the Author

Dr. **Peter L. Stiepleman**, the 2021 Missouri Superintendent of the Year, lives and works in the Pacific Northwest. He serves as an adviser to aspiring, new, and established superintendents and hosts a weekly podcast where he talks to current and former superintendents across the nation. To learn more, please visit www.peterstiepleman.com.